National Printing Company Publisher
Rossville, GA. 30741
Published in USA ISBN: 978-0-69211-307-3

Our prayer is that you enjoy this book by Grab a Prayer
Outreach Ministry Foundation Lord, grant this readers
power to increase their faith in You Lord, Amen.

Grab a Prayer

&

Hold on Tight

Kimberly Pittman-Porter

Truly I tell you, whatever you bind on earth will be bound
In heaven, and whatever you loose on earth will be loosed
in heaven.   Matthew 18:18-19 (KJV)

The Master's Words for Healing

GRAB
A
PRAYER
&
HOLD
ON
TIGHT

This is the LORD's doing, and it is wonderful to see.

Psalm 118:23 (NLT) Rejoice in the Lord, always again I say

rejoice   Philippians 4:4

I speak not by commandment, but I am testing the sincerity of

your love by the diligence of others, 2 Corinthians 8:8 (NKJV)

Confess your trespasses to one another, and pray for one

another, that you may be healed. The effective, fervent prayer

of a righteous man avails. James 5:16 (KJV)

Grab a Prayer & Hold on Tight

Presented To:

_____

From:

_____

Date:

_____

Notes/Comments:

_____

_____

_____

FOREWORD

Bishop Robert L. Williams

John Mark Missionary Baptist Church

4600 Workman Rd, Chattanooga, TN. 37407

"Daughter stay encouraged in all your endeavors,

you're doing a great job for the Lord.

Keep up the good work and stay encouraged".

Bishop Frederick Williams, Sr.

Gethsemane Worship Center

529 10th Ave. Albany, GA. 31705

"Continue to speak the word of hope!".

The late Pastor Richard Hewlett December 2011,

you received God's ultimate healing.

You are missed but never forgotten.

Greater Park City Mission Baptist Church

In the voice of the late Pastor Richard Hewlett

"You don't worry about what they say. Listen to God".

Pastor Eugene Stamper

Greater Park City Mission Baptist Church

224 Campton Street, Rossville GA. 30741

"Stay with the Lord and Keep God first".

ACKNOWLEDGMENTS

First and foremost, to the Most High God who is the lover
of my soul. This was the Lord's doing and it is marvelous
in our eyes. Mark 12:11. I give thanks and praise to God
in the highest. I was pregnant with this book for years.
The love of God has now birthed it to what is in your hands today.

To: My devoted friends and prayer partners
for giving me the encouragement to go on when the vision
was in the death, burial, and resurrection stage.

To: My children the late Appollonia Cherell Porter,
Jamell & Jamekra Porter Marsh, Terry Marsh Jr. (C-More,)
Crystal Sizemore Harris, and Tyrone Hawkins
for filling my life with joy, peace and happiness morning,
noon, and night. I am praying for God to move in their lives
like never before. Now the generational curse has been broken,
and I charge you to walk in the legacy of obedience.

To: My sisters and brother Linda Harris,
Roberta Davis (Rosie) Dr. Connie Hines-Brown and
Gary Hinton (San/Point. RIP Rest in Paradise)
for their prayers and faithfulness of fasting and praying
to bring this book to pass in my obedience by the will of God.

The Master's Words for Healing

To: My best friend Debbra Christopher for hours with me,
in and out of the will of God. Now into the marvelous
light of salvation through Christ Jesus our Lord and Savior,
We are now walking in the obedience of the Almighty God,
the Great I AM and to her mother Mrs. Alice Bonner who
always told us "Do what is right. God is watching".

To: My Bishop Fredrick Williams Sr. A man with a great vision
from God and one of the gatekeepers of the north.

To: My husband James Wesley Porter Jr. (Snap) for all the love
and support you have giving me over the years

To: My readers and supporters. I gratefully express my appreciation,
love, and support to all who have contributed to this production.
My prayers are that God blesses you by the daily prayers and
scripture in Grab a Prayer & Hold on Tight. I pray for your strength
in the Lord that you walk upright with mankind and God all the days
of your life, to serve God to the fullest in your daily living.

To: My sister-in-law Jeannette Dupree I love you with all my heart,
Thanks for all the encouragement over the years. God is Love.

To: My special beloved, Marvin Lee Kirk. Thank you,
Marvin, for dedicating your love and giving me a shoulder
to cry on, encouraging me when I didn't want to go forward,
and always letting me know how proud you are of my obedience
to our Lord and Saviour Jesus Christ.

To: My Spiritual Mom and Dad, Bishop Robert L. Williams
and First Lady Lucille Davis Williams of
John Mark Missionary Baptist Church,
4600 Workman Road, Chattanooga, TN. 37407
For the last five years you amazing angels,
have been so courageous, and obedient,
to the Will of God in my life. I will love you to infinity.

DEDICATION

To the Great I AM

This book is graciously dedicated first and foremost to

the lover of my soul, the Creator of Heaven and Earth,

the Great I AM, the Alpha and the Omega.

To my Lord and Savior Jesus Christ, the Son of the living God,

to the people of God and to the memory of my late mother and

earthly father, John and Dorothy Hines, who now have received

the ultimate Almighty healing on the other side, to eternal life.

To my late daughter Apollonia Porter, you carried your cross, my

daughter. To the other side, at the age of 4 months.

RIP my love, Mommy is on her way.

Believe

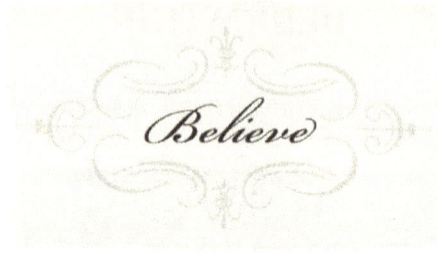

Use these layouts to open your own prayers.

Everlasting Father	Heavenly Father
How excellent is thy name	O Lord
Lord of Heaven and Earth	O Mighty God
Our Father	Prince of Peace
The Great I AM	The Mighty One
Thy Father of Glory	Thy Father of Grace
Thy Father of Heaven and Earth	Thy Father of Holiness
Thy Father of Joy	Thy Father of Love
Thy Father of Mercy	Thy Father of Peace
Thy Father of Truth	Thy Father of
Righteousness Yes Lord	Wonderful Counselor

Introduction

Miracle signs and wonders are loaded in this book. You

ever wondered why some people pray?

It's because of their belief. You ever wondered

why Jesus prayed in the garden of Gethsemane?

The bible says that he prayed, that God would take this

cup, from him but not his will; God's will.

We know now that God's will was for him to be borne by

a virgin, and to be crucified on a cross. That He may save

a dying world.

Letting every man-kind know that God Loves, Deliver,

and Save through His Words and Faith.

"Trust and Believe in God"

Grab a Prayer & Hold on Tight

Table of Contents

Powerful Prayers

33. The Elementary Prayer
34. The Father's Prayer
35. The Generational Curses
36. The Glory of the Lord
37. The Healed Eyes
38. The Mother's Prayer
39. The PM Prayers
40. The Prayer of Many Colors
41. The Pre-School Prayer
42. The Respectable and Honor Prayer
43. The Spirit of Alcohol
44. The Spirit of Autism
45. The Spirit of Constipation
46. The Spirit of COPD
47. The Spirit of STD's
48. The Spirit of Diabetes
49. The Spirit of Disorderly Behavior
50. The Spirit of Down syndrome
51. The Spirit of Drug Addiction
52. The Spirit of Shingles
53. The Spirit of Faith
54. The Spirit of Gambling
55. The Spirit of Gout
56. The Spirit of Guilt and Shame
57. The Spirit of Headaches
58. The Spirit of HIV/AIDS
59. The Spirit of Holiness
60. The Spirit of Homosexuality
61. The Spirit of Hypertension
62. The Spirit of Insomnia
63. The Spirit of Suicide
64. The Spirit of Loneliness
65. The Spirit of Love
66. The Spirit of Lupus Erythematous
67. The Spirit of Masturbation
68. The Spirit of Mental Imbalance

The 50 States Global Prayers

The Seven Continent Prayers

Global Prayers

The Powerful Prayers

Pain, has a way of crippling us, making us unable,
to stand or even walk. After all, we were created
to walk, in the likeness of God.
Don't let pain, stop you from trusting GOD.

1

Binding the Spirit of Addiction

The Father of Glory,

This addiction has me, by the heart. I have tried and tried

my God. to get delivered, set free and made whole again,

but this addiction has me down, and I can't seem to get free.

But today God, I trust in Your Word. Your word says,

who the Son set free is free indeed. I decree and declare,

that I am set free of this addiction.

This addiction has no control over me,

addiction be gone from me. From this day forward,

from the top of my head to the sole of my feet.

I am set free of this addiction. God, I choose You today,

to be my Lord and Savior, set me free, forgive me of all my sins.

I forgive anyone that has sin against me.

The Master's Words for Healing

I stand on the word in Matthew 18:18.

"Whatever you bind on earth will be bound in heaven,

and whatever you loose on earth will be loosed in heaven."

Spirit of addiction, I bind you up, and all your work on earth,

now you're bound in heaven. I loose the spirit of self-control

on earth, and now it is loose in heaven for me. I Thank God,

I'm no longer controlled by the spirit of addiction.

I prosper in the will of God. Spirit of addiction,

from this day forward, I am alive and set free get out of my mind,

get out of my body, and get out of my life!

I acknowledge addictions are diseases and by His stripes,

I know I am healed forever. Thank you, God Amen.

"All mankind is addicted to something or someone.
Whatever your addiction is, put that name of the addiction,
in front of the word Addiction, now say this prayer,
until you are free of that addiction, you need to be free,
healed, and delivered from this addiction."
By the Power of God, you are Healed, Amen.

2

Binding the Spirit of Obesity

Heavenly Father,

Thank You, for the breath that You have given me this day.

O Lord, rebuke me not in thine anger, neither chasten me

in thy hot displeasure. Have mercy upon me, O Lord;

for I am weak: O Lord, heal me; for my bones are vexed.

Lord thank You, for allowing me to be conscious,

of my obesity issue. I decree and declare,

that I would not consume high amounts of fats, and sugars.

I speak prophetically in my life. Lord let my hormones operate

the way You created them to be. I decree and declare, that

my fatty tissues are decreasing right now in the name of Jesus.

Heavenly Father, cause my body to function Supernaturally,

to burn more fatty tissues, that my body fat may decrease.

I declare, that I will stay active today, and keep a positive attitude.

I decree, that my insulin hormones are producing energy

effectively. I speak prophetically, to my hormone leptin,

cause me to be conscious and discipline myself concerning food.

Make me fully aware of when I should stop eating.

Lord help me follow a healthy eating plan.

Lord help me to make healthy food choices,

Lord help me keep my calorie needs and my family's calorie

needs in mind, and show me how to focus on Your Spirit,

and balance my energy in, and my energy out, to live a healthy

lifestyle. Teach me to focus on my portion size.

Let me be mindful of the portion sizes in fast food items.

Give me the power to select food, that will help me balance,

my energy in and out. Lord ignite me to be strong and active in

my daily activities. My eating habits today are lifestyle changes,

that will enrich me and my family from this day forward, Amen.

The Lord has heard my supplication.

The Lord will receive my prayer, and bless me,

Amen.

Psalms 6:9 (KJV)

3

Brain Tumor's

Thy Father of Mercy,

Blessed is the man that walketh not in the counsel of the ungodly,
nor standeth in the way of sinners, nor sitteth in the seat of the
scornful. But his delight is in the law of the Lord, and in his law
doth he meditates day and night. And he shall be like a tree
planted by the rivers of water, that bringeth forth his fruit in his
season; his leaf also shall not wither, and whatsoever he doeth
shall prosper. The ungodly shall perish; The ungodly are not so:
but are like the chaff which the wind driveth away. Therefore,
the ungodly shall not stand in the judgment, nor sinners in the
congregation of the righteous. Primary Central, Nervous System
Pituitary, become normal as God created you to be,
in Jesus name. Headaches, numbness, and tingling be gone
from my body. I am made whole. I decree and declare that there
will be no seizures in this body. I speak prophetically that this
brain tumor is now shrinking, Amen.   Psalms 1:1-5 (KJV)

4

Breast Cancer

Thy Father of Peace,

Grant me peace that I may endure until my healing come,

On the day I called, you answered me; my strength of soul You

increased. Trust in the LORD with all your heart, and do not lean

on your own understanding. In all your ways acknowledge him,

and he will make straight your paths. God, You, said come to me,

all who labor and are heavy laden, and I will give you rest. Take

my yoke upon you, and learn from me, for I am gentle and lowly in

heart, and you will find rest for your souls. I come to You God

with all that

I am. Heal me that I may give glory to Your name. I will let all

know that I live because You care. You are God all by Yourself, I

choose to worship and praise You. I decree and declare that there

is no uncontrolled growth of the breast cells in this body.

Malignant tumors dry up in Jesus name, Amen.

Psalms 138:3, Proverbs 3:5-6, Matthew 11:28-29 (KJV)

God Hears Prayer

5

Cancerous Diseases

The Great I AM,

Have mercy on me for this disease is claiming my body,

now my Lord Your grace is sufficient for me.

You love me so much. That You sent Your son to die on the cross

for me, and by His Stripes. I am healed, I decree, and declare,

that all the cancerous cell in my body, are drying up in Jesus name,

no weapon formed against me shall prosper.

I plead the blood of Jesus, over my mind body and soul.

Thank You, Lord, Amen.

6

Commanding Your Morning

Heavenly Father,

I am a joint heir with Jesus Christ, my bloodline is contagiously

blessed. I declare that You are Lord of lords, King of kings.

Your Word will not come back to You void.

My DNA spells GOD, Great Ordained Destiny.

I speak this morning to declare Your glory! Hallelujah.

I repent of all my sins, and ask God for forgiveness,

for any transgressions that might hinder my blessing.

I forgive anyone that has transgressed against me.

I declare, that this morning is a new day-old thing's has

Passed away, all things become new.

Grab a Prayer & Hold on Tight

I command this day to cooperate, with Your purpose and plan

for me and my family life. We are covered with Your anointing.

Your Spirit dwells in us. My Lord, I come in agreement with You,

and heaven, my appointed time is in Your hands.

When I pray provisions materialize, my prayers declare Your

glory. I declare my stomach is filled with my destiny.

Your extraordinary plan is being executed in my life right now.

I command access to my assignments this day.

Open doors of opportunity, for miracles, signs, and wonders,

My Lord channels of love, joy, peace, kindness, goodness,

faithfulness, gentleness, self-control, and strengthen me for the

longsuffering. Closed the doors that would cause me,

to stumble and fall. Teach me Your ways, that I may follow,

order my steps for You are my God. I will conduct my affairs,

with Your guidance. I declare, that Your Anointing flows through

me uncontaminated, and unhindered.

I command this morning to conceive right now, my inheritance

and give power to me for healing, deliverance, breakthroughs, and revelations. Grant me peace, love, joy, faith, fruitful

relationships and resourceful finances. I am daily loaded with

Your benefits, my destiny is achievable, and it shall become

inevitable and legendary, for the Glory of God! I speak to the

winds, earthly wind from the East, West, South, and North I

command you to bring forth heavenly instructions on my behalf.

I claim every assignment in my life that God has given me today

completed in Jesus name.

Now my Lord as my praise enters Your Holy Throne

before I am finished speaking. You, my Lord, will answer my call;

You will make a road in the wilderness for me, and a river in the

desert. I command this morning to spring forth my assignments

right now. I declare accomplishment in Your will for my life this

day. I shall declare Your glory and praises all the days of my life.

I renounce burdens and everything that so easy besets me,

I loose the spirit of liberty. Holy Spirit have your way in this place

today. I loose all Unforgiveness, envy, and strife in my heart.

I replace them with Your love and Your yoke; for it is easy.

Grab a Prayer & Hold on Tight

I put on beauty for ashes, the oil of joy for mourning.

I loose all soul ties that surrender my bondage to the kingdom of

darkness. Satan, you have no power in my life.

My body is the temple of the Holy Spirit.

I decree and declare that I am contagiously blessed,

Jehovah- Jireh You have and always will provide for me.

I declare that I am blessed, yes contagiously blessed.

Every evil agenda assigned to me is now becoming frustrated

in the soil of conception and it will never prevail. Infirmity and

sickness are far from me. I am made whole in Jesus name,

Jesus took the sting out of death and by His stripes, I am healed.

I am blessed generations to come. I have excellent health;

my labor is not in vain. I have the mind of Christ Jesus.

I am learning to manifest kingdom principles and powers,

I am becoming wiser, faster than lighting spreading the word

of God. When I pray provision materializes.

I have the multi-billionaire mindset for kingdom ideas

and inventions. My steps are ordered by God.

The Master's Words for Healing

I declare that I am a representative for the kingdom of God

enter-acting with programs and activities to enrich the kingdom

of Heaven. I don't only make money

I also give money for the kingdom of heaven enrichment.

That a dying soul may know that You are God.

I declare that I have a great inheritance through Christ Jesus,

my children, children for generations to come shall partake of this

inheritance. I vow to be a good stewardess for the body of Christ

and my family. My Lord praise shall come forth from my lips all

day long. Let me forever maintain a blameless heart, let my hands

stay clean. Let Your blessings be with me forever.

I Thank You, Lord, for Your provision and empowerment.

I seal this prayer in heaven and footnote it in hell, it becomes law.

in the name of Jesus, Amen.

To God be the Glory, Shalom.

And ye shall know the truth, and the truth shall make you free.

7

Compulsive Sex Addiction Spirit

The Father of Mercy,

You have seen all my sins, You, are a God that forgives all sins.

My Lord, I am so sorry that I have let my flesh rule over me.

I humble myself before Your Holy Throne, help me with this

desire; Your word says that you will give us the desire of our heart.

I know that you have not given me this desire but it is of the evil

one. Therefore, it is not of you and I want no part of it in my life.

I repent of all my sins, hide not Your face from me,

but lean Your ear to my call. for I am Your child and You are my

God, there is none like you. Many sorrows shall be to the wicked:

but he that trusteth in the Lord, mercy shall compass him about.

Thank You, God for Your Forgiveness, Amen.

Psalm 32:10. (KJV)

**Praying is the way I give my children back to God.
In other words, I start saying what God says,
about my Children, before I see it come to pass.
God works through our faith, it's how faith works.**

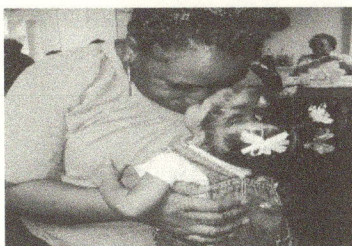

8

Confession Scriptures over Your Children

Thy Father of Heaven and Earth,

I declare my children are blessed. As it is written,

"I have made you a father of many nations."

In the presence of Him whom he believed God,

who gives life to the dead, and calls those things which

do not exist as though they did. I "speak those things are not as if

they are". My children are blessed; they are beautifully made in

God's image. They are blessed in their going and they're coming

out.

Grab a Prayer & Hold on Tight

God shall protect them I refuse to be afraid for my children safety.

I surround them with faith hope and the love of God.

I speak prophetically into their life they are healthy, happy.

and protected by God.

I speak blessings over my relationship with my children,

we shall be able to communicate with each other with a

sound mind, and the love, and the power of God.

I decree and declare that my house is filled with peace, love, and

holiness. I declare that my children know who God is and love

God. They are becoming sensitive to the voice of God,

They are hungry for the things of God. And obey the Holy Spirit.

Revelation from God flows to them and they see and understand

spiritual things. They know what God has called them to be,

and they are able to complete the assignment.

God bless me with the wisdom to bless and help my children,

Amen.   Romans 4:1. (KJV)

9

Crohn's Disease
Thy Father of Love,

Thank You, Lord, how sweet is Your name, blessed is the

Most High God. That created the heavens and the earth.

Our Father in heaven, Hallowed be Your name,

Your Kingdom come. Your Will be done on earth as it is in

heaven. Give us this day our daily bread. And forgive us our

debts, as we forgive our debtors. And do not lead us into

temptation, but deliver us from the evil one. For Yours is the

kingdom and the power and the glory forever. Amen. Be glad in

the Lord, and rejoice,

ye righteous: and shout for joy, all ye that are upright in heart.

I decree and declare that my immune system cooperates with

God's plans for my life. I decree and declare, that the lining

of the bowel is flowing normal, and there is no inflammation

in my body. Thank You, Lord Amen.

Matthew 6:10, Psalm 32:11 (KJV)

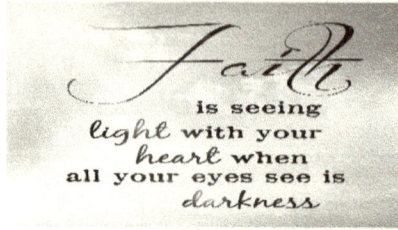

Faith is seeing
light with your
heart when
all your eyes see is
darkness

10

My Daily Confession by Faith

The Father of Love,

I pray that Your Purpose and plan for my life be manifested

this day. I am a child of the Most High God,

I am a joint heir with Jesus Christ appointed for this time.

I am a chosen generation, a royal priesthood, a holy nation,

a peculiar people. I walk upright before God and man.

If God be for me then who can be against me.

I loose the spirit of fear for God has not given me the spirit

of fear, but of power, love and a sound mind.

I have the mind of Christ. I speak the truth and declare that

no weapon formed against me shall prosper.

As I pray, provision materializes and every tongue that rises against me You shall condemn. This is my heritage.

My righteousness is from God. I am the head and not the tail

above and not beneath. I am more than a conqueror.

I declare that the West winds of replenishment

are at my door, replenishing me. The North winds of abundance

are chasing me and they have consumed me

I have more than enough. The South winds of restoration

penetrate every pore in my body and I am restored.

The East winds of judgment subdue my enemies.

And they are destroyed. I am contagiously blessed.

Satan the Lord rebukes you concerning me. What God has blessed

no one can curse. Those that bless me shall be blessed and those

that curse me shall be cursed. I will love the Lord with all my

heart, soul, and mind. I will love my neighbor as myself.

When my enemies come against me the righteousness

of God will cause them to flee in seven different directions.

Every evil assignment and negative word was ever spoken

over me is now broken through the word and power of God

in generations to come. I come in the name of Jesus.

Lord forgive me of all my sins.

I forgive anyone that has sinned against me.

I renew my mind in the Word of God.

I am chosen to be blessed. It is written I am a child of God,

saved by grace, redeemed by the blood of Christ,

forgiven of all my sins which are sealed with the Spirit of God.

I am an ambassador of Christ.

I humble myself under the hand of God.

I cast all my cares upon the Lord for He cares for me.

I am established by God.

All my affairs will be under His directions.

This I declare, now God will establish it for me.

To God be the Glory Forever and ever, Amen.

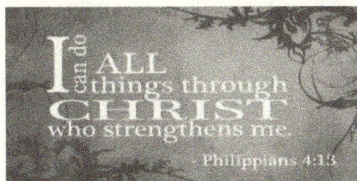

11

The Declaration Prayer

Thy Father of Glory,

The kingdom of God suffers violence and the violent take it

back by force, the gates of hell shall not prevail against Gods

church. Satan the Lord rebukes you concerning me and all my

activities today. I speak prophetically I decree and declare that

I consecrate myself to the Lord for His good pleasure.

I receive the oil of joy and fresh anointing that empowers

me to be effective today.

I decree and declare that I shall not be distracted by any device

of the enemy, but I shall receive peace, power, deliverance,

breakthroughs, and victory in every dimension of my life.

I will do the will of the Lord;

I repent of all my sins and ask God to forgive me.

Grab a Prayer & Hold on Tight

I take authority in Jesus name; I confess all sins that have given the enemy legal rights over me and my family.

I command every organized strategy of the host of darkness enforcing any curses of harm over me and my family life to be destroyed. I command every master spirit or controlling power responsible for enforcing harm over me and my family to be arrested and their assignments have been terminated through the blood and power of Jesus Christ.

I command the anointing for multiple breakthroughs to come upon me and consume my life.

Thank You, Lord, because Jesus is my Lord, Amen.

12
Healed from Sexual Abuse

Thy Father of Peace,

Lord show me how to forgive, them that sexually abused me.
That I may be healed. To You my Lord, I will trust for my healing,
to You I will cry out, O LORD my Rock: Do not be silent to me,
lest, if You are silent to me, I become like those who go down to
the pit. Hear the voice of my supplications when I cry to You when
I lift up my hands toward Your holy sanctuary.

Do not take me away with the wicked and with the workers of
iniquity, who speak peace to their neighbors, but evil is in their
hearts. Give them according to their deeds, and according to the
wickedness of their endeavors; give them according to the work of
their hands; render to them what they deserve. Because they do not
regard the works of the LORD, nor the operation of His hands,
He shall destroy them and not build them up. Blessed be the
LORD because He has heard the voice of my supplications!

The LORD is my strength and my shield; my heart trusted in Him,

and I am helped; therefore, my heart greatly rejoices, and with my

song, I will praise Him. The LORD is their strength, and He is the

saving refuge of His anointed. Save Your people, and bless

Your inheritance; Shepherd them also, and bear them up forever.

Praise ye the LORD. I will praise the LORD with my whole heart,

in the assembly of the upright, and in the congregation.

The works of the LORD are great, sought out of all them that

have pleasure therein. His work is honorable and glorious:

and his righteousness endureth forever. He hath made his

wonderful works to be remembered: the LORD is gracious

and full of compassion. He hath given meat unto them that fear

him: he will ever be mindful of his covenant. He hath showed his

people the power of His works, that He may give them the heritage

of the heathen. The works of his hands are verity and judgment;

All his commandments are sure. They stand fast for ever and ever

and are done in truth and uprightness. He sent redemption unto

His people: He hath commanded His covenant forever:

holy and reverend is his name. The fear of the LORD is the

beginning of wisdom: a good understanding have all they that do

His commandments: His praise endureth forever, Amen.

Psalms 28:7-9 (KJV)

Denial is not failure it's Practice

13

Healed from the Spirit of Denial

Thy Father of Truth,

I break the spirit of denial over my life, and forever more.

Spirit of denial get out of my life, you have no authority over me.

I understand that denial is not final, therefore my God shall

supply all my needs according to his riches and Glory by Christ

Jesus. I received my approval from God he has made me in His

image and I am beautifully made. There is nothing wrong with me.

What the enemy meant for bad God will turn it around for my

good. I break the power of any demonic curses; any demonic

people trying to deny the purpose and plans for my life.

I will accomplish what God has called me to do.

In Jesus Mighty name, Amen.   Philippians 4:19 (KJV)

14

Healing Fetal Abnormalities

How Excellent is Thy Name,

You are my God, I put my trust in You, for it is You O Lord

that gives life. I pray that you strengthen my child,

that I may raise him or her to be what You have called them

to be before the foundation of the earth. Create in me a clean

heart and renew a right spirit.

O Lord the God of our Lord Jesus Christ, the Father of glory,

may give to you the spirit of wisdom and revelation in the

knowledge of Him, the eyes of your understanding being

enlightened; that you may know what the hope of His calling is,

what are the riches of the glory of His inheritance in the saints,

and what is the exceeding greatness of His power toward us who

believe, according to the working of His mighty power.

Lord heal any fetal abnormalities that I may raise the child as You,

would have me to. Lord, I Thank You for this Healing Amen.

Ephesians 1:17-19 (KJV)

15

Healing for Abnormal Heart

Thy Father of Love,

God, I cried with a loud voice, saying, You, are our God

that sits on the throne, hear our crying hearts that as the report

has come down concerning an abnormal heart. Unto You God

our hearts belong. Blessed be the name of God,

the Creator of Heaven and Earth.

Spirit of congested heart failure, heart attack, tetralogy of Fallot,

ductus arteriosus, endocarditis and all congenital heart disease;

become normal from this day forward. Let any abnormal illness

in this body become supernatural healed. Blessings, and glory,

and wisdom, and thanksgiving, and honor, and power, and might,

be unto our God forever and ever. Amen.

The Master's Words for Healing

And one of the elders answered, saying unto me,

What are these which are arrayed in white robes?

and whence came they? And I said unto him, Sir, thou knowest.

And he said to me, these are they which came out of great

tribulation, and have washed their robes, and made them

white in the blood of the Lamb. Therefore, are they before the

throne of God, and serve him day and night in his temple: and he

that sitteth on the throne shall dwell among them.

They shall hunger no more, neither thirst anymore;

neither shall the sun light on them, nor any heat.

 For the Lamb which is in the midst of the throne shall feed

them, and shall lead them unto living fountains of waters:

and God shall wipe away all tears from their eyes.

Lord Thank You for wiping away all my tears, Amen.

Rev 7:11-17 (KJV)

16

Healing for Kidney and Liver Disease

Everlasting Father,

I speak prophetically to my liver and kidney.

You play a vital role in my body functions,

I decree and declare that you are made whole,

the way God intended you to perform in the beginning of old.

I decree and declare all fluid that is not the design protocol

for my liver, and kidney to dry up right now.

I decree and declare that my body is being made whole from

the inside out. I am healed in Jesus mighty name.

Trust in the Lord with all your heart, and lean not on your

own understanding; Hallelujah,

Thank You, Lord.

Proverbs 3:5 (KJV)

17

Healing of the Ears

Heavenly Father,

Then, looking up to heaven, He sighed, and said to

him, "Ephphatha," that is, "Be opened."

Immediately his ears were opened, and the impediment

of his tongue was loosed, and he spoke plainly.

I come in the name of Jesus,

eardrum "Ephphatha," "Ephphatha," "Ephphatha,".

Meaning "Be opened.", "Be opened.", "Be opened."

Eardrum in the mighty name of Jesus.

The tympanic membrane, and the external ear Open

by the Power of God. Now function, and transmit

sound from the air to the ossicles inside the middle ear,

and then to the oval window in the fluid-filled cochlea.

That I may hear what the Spirit of the Lord is saying to

the church. In Jesus name. Amen.   Mark 7:34-35

(KJV)

18

The Family Prayer

Thy Father of Love,

Lord thank You for our family. Teach us to do good and not evil

to each other. Lord, I pray You build us up where we are weak.

Thank You for the food on our table, the roof over our heads,

and the clothes on our backs.

Lord guide and protect us to do Your Will each day.

Empower each one of us to be what You have called us to be,

Heavenly Father, teach us to Love and Forgive as You do.

Amen. Thank You, Lord.

Believe

With God all things are possible!

19

I am the Abuser Forgive Me, Lord

Thy Father of Mercy,

I am the one that has abused people in my life.

Forgive me of all my sins, and I forgive anyone that has

sinned against me. Show me Your Way, Lord,

Teach Me How to Love how to cherish, honor and

respect people in my life. Lord, I pray that they forgive

me for the abuse I've done in their life.

Have mercy on me. Give them the forgiveness in your

heart to forgive me for all I have caused.

God Your word says. Let us, therefore, come boldly

unto the throne of grace, that we may obtain mercy,

and find grace to help in time of need. Lord,

I am coming to You, Thank You for forgiving me,

Amen.   Hebrews 4:16 (KJV)

20

Ovarian Cancer

Thy Father of Peace,

I decree and declare that there are no abnormal signs

in my body. Fatigue, upset stomach, abnormal bloating,

back pain, constipation, and swelling be gone

and dry up in my body. Your assignment is terminated

in my life, in the mighty name of Jesus. Halleluiah,

Jesus board my infirmities and by His stripes,

I declare my healing. Thy Father of Glory,

I claim my healing today. You are my God and

I Thank You for healing me Amen.

21

Proclaimed Normal Hyperlipidemia

O Mighty God,

Thank You, God, for being the Great Healer

that You are. Thy Father of Glory,

Thy Father of Peace have mercy on me.

Supernaturally bring my cholesterol level to what You

would have it to be.

I am healed and made whole in Jesus name,

Amen.

22

The Salvation Prayer

Dear Friend,

If you decided to receive the Lords Salvation you just made the greatest decision of your life. If you need to rededicate your life now is the time to come back home where you belong as it is written: "There is none rightcous, no, not one, Just say this simple prayer and mean it in your heart. Then the Lord Jesus Christ will come into your heart. He will seal you with the Holy Spirit and the Holy Spirit will guide you into all truth.

The Romans Road Prayer for Salvation

3:10 As it is written: "There is none righteous, no, not one;

"The pure facts of our sins" 3:23 "For all have sinned and come short of the glory of God,"

"We need Salvation" 6:23

For the wages of sin is death, but the gift of God is eternal

life through Jesus Christ our Lord.

"The Promise of God's Eternal Life". 10:9

That if thou shalt confess with thy mouth the Lord Jesus,

and shalt believe in thine heart that God hath raised Him

from the dead, thou shalt be saved.

"The Gift to Mankind" 10:10 For with the heart man believeth unto

righteousness, and with the mouth, confession is made unto

salvation. "Our Responsibility" 10:13

For whosoever shall call upon the name of the Lord shall be saved.

"This is the Promise of Salvation"

Heavenly Father,

"I am a sinner forgive me of all my sins. Have mercy on me,

Lord. I believe Your Son died on the cross for all my sins.

Come into my heart I receive you as my Lord and Savior,

seal me with the Holy Spirit. I vow to serve You Lord

all the days of my life, in Jesus name, Amen."

Welcome to the family of God! You are now a child of the

Most High God. "Therefore, if anyone is in Christ he is a

new creature: old things have passed away;

Behold all things have become new." 2 Corinthians 5:17.

Don't let Satan; others or you condemn yourself of your past sins.

God has forgiven you. Now forgive yourself and ask others

to forgive you, don't lose hope or faith on this journey it just

may get worse before it gets better.

I can promise you one thing Satan, is mad as Hell,

because you have chosen to live for Christ.

He will fight to discourage you and he will try to win your soul

back. Get in the Word of God, stay prayed up and get in a

good church home. The effective fervent prayer of the righteous

avails much. Trust the Holy Spirit to guide you on this journey,

remember you have citizenship in the kingdom of heaven:

your victory is inevitable, Amen. Read the book, the Holy Bible,

it tells you in the end, you Win. Even unto death you are, a

Winner walk in victory in Jesus Name, Amen.

23

Spouse Abuse

Heavenly Father,

This is my prayer; vindicate me, O Lord for I have walked

with my spouse. The time has come when it must stop.

I can take no more Lord, You, are my redeemer;

have mercy on me. I have trusted in my spouse and

we have walked in iniquity, shame is on my head. For the love,

I have for them has redeemed me powerless.

All power belongs to You and the place where Your Glory dwells.

I have survived so much; I am not ignorant of Your Power.

I have heard of Your miracles, signs, and wonders,

I acknowledge You are my Lord, and Savior come rescue me,

less I go the pit where darkness shall engulf my soul.

I wait patiently for the Lord, for You, my God will answer my

prayers. You will bring me out of this horrible bondage,

Lord, I come in the scroll of the book: it is written of me,

Lord do not rebuke me in Your wrath nor chasten me in Your

hot displeasure because of my sin. I am feeble and severely

broken. I groan because of the turmoil of my heart, Lord all my

desire is before You; and my spouse's sins are not hidden from

Your eyes. Order my steps, make me not mute, and open my

mouth to declare Your words. Grant me spiritual warfare for my

spouse; break the abuse spirit in my spouse. Thank You for Your

deliverance in the face of my enemy. I speak to the spirit of abuse,

I pull this stronghold down. I root up bitterness; I curse your

assignment in my spouse life. You have no victory here Satan,

death will not grip my marriage. God's anointing breaks the back

of your hold on my spouse. I plead the blood of Jesus over this

relationship I curse the root of every lie spoken in my spouse's

mind. I decree and declare that my spouse shall operate in the

The Master's Words for Healing

order of God. I bind every negative word that comes from my

spouse's mouth; every trick of the enemy will fail.

I curse the spirit of division and free the spirit of unity.

Our communion is whole I will walk upright before the

Lord and He will deliver me from this for this too shall pass.

I am blessed in my home and in the city; no weapon formed

against me shall prosper. Every evil conspiracy act behind

dark doors will come to the light in Jesus name.

The spirit of betrayal, I cut you off our lives.

You will never again oppress me. I loose the spirit of holiness

from this day, forth. Satan, I unplug your power,

I decree and declare that you are having a blackout in my life.

Everything that is associated with you is corrupted,

I command the Holy Spirit to flow through me, and Holy Spirit

I give You liberty in my life right now. Lord is my shepherd;

I shall not want He makes me to lie down in green pastures;

He leads me beside the still waters. He restores my soul;

He leads me in the paths of righteousness For His name's sake.

Grab a Prayer & Hold on Tight

Yea, though I walk through the valley of the shadow of death,

I will fear no evil; For You are with me; Your rod and Your staff,

they comfort me. You prepare a table before me in the presence

of my enemies; You anoint my head with oil, my cup runs over.

Surely goodness and mercy shall follow me all the days of my life,

and I will dwell in the house of the Lord forever.

The Lord God is Jehovah-Jireh, my great provider.

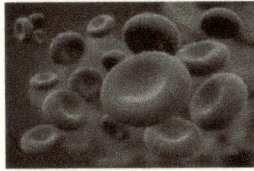

24

Supernatural Blood Cell Reproduction

O Mighty God,

Red blood cell I decree and declare that you are supernaturally increased, I speak in the authority of the Most High God. Hemoglobin carry oxygen from my lungs to the rest of my body and supernaturally return carbon dioxide from my body to my lungs. Heavenly Father, I decree and declare that my white blood cells supernaturally function to help protect my body from any infection and any foreign materials. That would cause my body not to operate, the way God intended it to be. In the mighty name of Jesus Christ Amen.

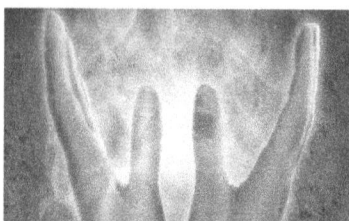

25

Terminal Illnesses

Thy Father of Peace,

You are Jehovah Rapha – The Lord that Heals. The healer of my

soul, You, are Jehovah – Jeri my grate provider there is none like

you. Come and rescuer me form the gravel.

Lord, You, said If thou wilt diligently hearken to the voice of the

LORD thy God, and will do that which is right in His sight,

and wilt give ear to His commandments and keep all His statutes,

I will put none of these diseases upon thee, which I have brought

upon the Egyptians: for I am the LORD that healeth thee.

As of today, according to Your words, I will do all that You have

command. Heal thy body right now, that I may know that

You are the true and living God. Strongman, terminal illness,

The Master's Words for Healing

in the authority of God.

I terminate the assignments of illness in this body.

Lord, Thank You for Your amazing grace that passes to all

generations. I speak prophetically to my body right now.

Hear the Words of the Lord and receive the healing from

the Words of the Lord, Body you are healed, now receive and

respond on the Words of the Lord.

I command my body to perform the way God created it to function.

All my pain is gone behold the Lamb of God.

But He was wounded for our transgressions,

He was bruised for our iniquities;

The chastisement for our peace was upon Him,

And by His stripes, we are healed.

In Jesus name, Amen.

Isaiah 53:3, Exodus 15:26. (KJV)

26

The Am Prayer

Thy Father of Glory

How excellent is Thy Name; Almighty God, the one who created

heaven and earth. The beginning and the end. The Great I Am,

I come before Your Holy Throne, my God.

To ask You to bless this day. Lord bless my family and equip those

that I may encounter today, to be receptive to Your word. O my

Lord, have Your way in my life. I give You all the glory and all the

praises. You so rightfully deserve all the honor. Protect me,

God, close the doors that will cause me to stumble and fall.

Build Me Up where I'm weak, that I may do Great and Mighty

things in the land of the living, and I promise to give You honor,

glory, and praises.   Hallelujah and Amen.

27

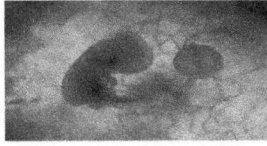

The Blessing of the Womb Fertilization

Thy Father of Love

Thank you for loving me, Lord, fertilize my womb, to

conceive the child. That You have for me, before the

beginning of time. Now, my Lord, I pray for my womb

to become fertile; that I may conceive a child.

I speak prophetically, to my spiritual womb line up

with the will of God for my life. Now my Lord,

I call those things that are not; as if they are. My body is

productive, and fertile to conceive my child. All praise

belongs to God. Have Your way God in my life right

now. In the Mighty name of Jesus Christ of Nazareth.

Amen.

28

The Broken Hearted

Thy Father of Peace

Lord, I come to You now broken-hearted,

for You alone know my pain and all that I have suffered.

They hurt me without a cause, remove this pain deep

within my heart. That I may live again in peace, hope,

faith, and happiness. God remember the days of old,

is Your promise to Abraham, that You will bless his

seeds? God, I'm Your child one of the seeds of Abraham.

Come rescue me, deliver me in the time of need.

For I need You, Lord, right now. Thank You, for saving

my life. Thank You, my God, for healing me, Thank

You, for mending my heart, I trust You, Lord.

In Jesus Name, Amen.

With God all things are possible
Matthew 19:26

29

The Child Sexual Abused Prayer

Thy Father of Glory

My God, my God, I know that you have not forsaken me.

I am the child that was abused, there was no one there to

protect me. The one that sexually abused me,

my God how do I ask you to have mercy upon them.

Show me, Lord. When I harbor un-forgiveness in

my heart for them. Show me my God and Deliver

Me from this un-forgiveness, deliver me from this pain,

from this shame, and this disgrace that is in my heart.

There has been a horrific thing that happened to me.

but my God I trust and believe in Your holy word.

Your Word says, my God, that you have forgiven me

of all my sins. Now my Lord ease my heart God that

I may forgive my abuser. Teach Me, Lord, how to

forgive, how to love your way. For this burden of abuse

that is upon me, it is too heavy for me and

I can no longer carry this burden. So, this day,

I cast my burdens upon you, Lord, for I know my God

You care for me. God, You, did not cause this to happen

to me but my God You can turn it around for Your good.

let me not be ashamed to let mankind know, that sexual

abuse is wrong. God turn my tears into Joy.

I take a leap of faith and forgive them in my heart, in my

mind, in my body, and in my soul, I forgive them in my

heart, that I may be made whole to love the way God

loves. Thank you, God, for loving me,

Thank You, Lord for saving me. I am at peace,

and I am free because who the Son set free is free indeed.

I claim Liberty over this situation Satan get out of my

life. In Jesus name, Amen.

30

The Childs Prayer

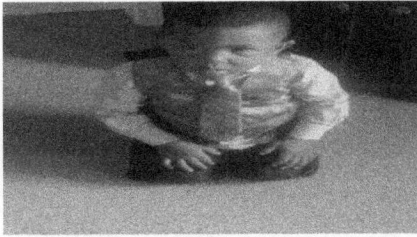

My God,

Hear my prayer for I am your child,

protect me all the days of my life.

Teach me Your ways God, that I may follow.

My mind my body and, my soul belongs to God.

I decree and declare that Jesus is Lord. Amen.

31

The College Students Prayer

O Mighty God,

I know that you see all things, have your way on this campus.

Lord, let no harm come near me. Cancel every assignment,

that the enemy has placed on this school.

Let all that come to harm this school fall in their own demise.

Lord help me to speak encouraging words throughout my day.

When apologies are needed give me the strength to do it quickly.

Give me an ear to listen, to learn, and understand.

Help me to encourage, equip, and empower, others for Your glory.

Teach me, Lord, to be slow to anger,

I decree and declare that there will be no shootings on this campus,

Amen.

32

My Daily Declaration Prayer

Thy Father of Heaven and Earth,

I speak prophetically right now, I decree and declare that Jesus is Lord. For the bible says that the kingdom of God suffers violence and the violent take it back by force. For I am the righteous of God

Therefore, the gates of hell shall not prevail against me or my family. Satan the Lord rebukes you concerning me and

all my activities today. I speak prophetically I decree and declare that Jesus is Lord. The oil of joy refreshes me I am anointing and empowers to do the will of God. I am loaded daily with benefits

no weapon formed against me shall prosper. I decree and declare that I shall not be distracted by the enemy, But I shall receive peace, power, and victory in every dimension of my life.

Grab a Prayer & Hold on Tight

I will do the will of the Lord; I take authority in Jesus name; I confess all sins that have given the enemy legal rights over me and my family. I forgive anyone that has sin against me, in the Mighty name of Jesus. I command every organized strategy of darkness enforcing, any curses or harm over me and my family life to be destroyed. I command every master spirit or controlling powers responsible, for discord over me and my family, to be arrested and their assignments have been terminated through the blood and power of Jesus Christ.

I command the anointing for multiple breakthroughs to come upon me and consume my life. Thank You, Lord,

for my life Jesus is Lord, Amen.

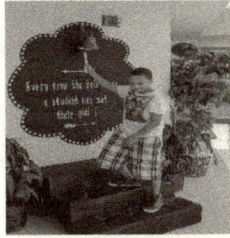

33

The Elementary Prayer

The Great I AM

Thank You, God for loving me,

Thank You, for Your Protection.

Help me to love as You, love.

Help me to say sorry when I have made a mistake.

Teach me to listen and, learn.

Show me Your, ways that I may follow,

You, all the days of my life.

Teach me not to bully and not to be bullied by others,

Let my school be safe today, Amen.

34

The Father's Prayer

Heavenly Father,

Have mercy on my children keep them safe all-day long.

Let their decisions give You the Most High respect,

teach them to trust You forever, and owe no man anything

but to love them. Grant them guidance, love, and respect.

Give them the ability of good leadership. Show them, Lord,

how to love themselves and never forget who God is to them.

Protect them, Lord, as You have always protected Your children.

Let them not turn to the right, nor to the left, but in all things

Let them acknowledge, and follow You. Put Your angels in charge

of them and protect them, every step of the way;

that it may be well with You My Lord. For this day,

I give them back to You, have Your way.

The Master's Words for Healing

Hear my prayer, O LORD and give ear unto my cry;

hold not thy peace at my tears: for I am a stranger with thee,

and a sojourner, as all my fathers were.

Let thine ear now be attentive, and thine eyes open,

that thou mayest hear the prayer of thy servant,

which I pray before thee now, day and night,

for the children of Israel thy servants, and confess the sins

of the children of Israel, which we have sinned against thee:

both I and my father's house have sinned.

Now from this day forward,

Me and my house will serve the Lord.

I seal this prayer in the name of Jesus,

 it becomes law in heaven and earth, Amen.

Psalm. 39.1 1-13, Nehemiah 1:6

35

The Generational Curses

Thy Father of Righteousness,

Lord I Proclaim, that our generation is not dysfunctional.

I take authority this day, and every day.

I cast down every imagination and every high thing that exalts

itself, above the knowledge of God.

I decree and declare that every generational curse is broken.

There is no conflict that God cannot resolve.

I come in the authority of the Holy book, that was given to us.

Our DNA is carrying every genetics cell, through the blood of

Jesus Christ, becoming supernatural whole, to God be the glory.

Lord, I surrender all to You; therefore, through the Power of God,

every generational curse is broken by the Power of God.

The Master's Words for Healing

I submit to You all that I am and all that I will ever become.

Lord Your Word says if I resist the devil, he will flee from me.

Thy Father of Glory, I Confess all my sins and the sins of my

parents. Lord, I forgive any sins of my parents. I take authority that

is given to me in the volume of the Holy Book. I break any soul

ties of ungodliness with any mankind. I will do the will of the

Lord. Through the Power of God, I Break the generational curse of

the demon control and any demoniac force; over my family

 bloodline. I command every demon and demonic powers

enforcing havoc over my generation and four generations to come

to leave me and my family along. In the name of Jesus Christ be

gone forever. Thank You, Lord, for I know that Your Words are

true. But because of His great love for us, God, who is rich in

mercy, made us alive with Christ, even when we were dead in

transgressions—it is by grace, you have been saved.

Set free to do the Will of God for your generations Amen.

Ephesians 2:4-5

36

The Glory of the Lord

Thy Father of Glory,

All glory belongs to You, Halleluiah, Halleluiah, Halleluiah,

to Your Holy Name. I choose to praise You right now.

This is the day that the Lord has made I will rejoice and be glad

in it and again I say rejoice. Thank You for Your amazing grace

Your mercy endures to all generations You are my God

I am Your child let me forever be blessed.

The Glory of the Lord is in this place, it's in this house today.

Thank You for Your anointing in Jesus name,

Thank You for Your Words they are life to me and death to others;

Let Your Glory rise upon me.

Let Your loving-kindness forever be in my face.

Lend Your ear to my call for I am Your child.

Forgive me of all my sins; my God have mercy on me.

The Lord has sworn by His right hand and by the arm of His

strength saying, "Surely I will no longer give your grain as food for your enemies, and the sons of the foreigner shall not

drink your new wine. For your labor is not in vain." Isaiah 62:8.

The Glory of the Lord shall go forth; He will remember

my rebellions no more. With His glorious arm, He will keep me.

Let the Glory of the Lord be with me right now.

Blessed is the Glory of the Lord for He has heard my cry.

Blessed is the Glory of the Lord for His mercy endures forever.

Blessed is the Glory of the Lord for He established the just.

I decree and declare a new season, of prophetic fulfillment and

manifestation to take effect in my life today for God's glory.

To God be the glory forever and ever, Amen.

37

The Healed Eyes

Thy Father of Heaven and Earth,

Deal bountifully with Your servant, That I may live and keep Your Word. Open my eyes, that I may see Wondrous things from Your law. I am a stranger in the earth; Do not hide Your commandments from me. Psalms 119:17-19. Let me not see illusion,

but let these eyes be open unto Your Holy Word.

And Jesus said, "For judgment, I came into this world, so that those who do not see may see, and that those who see may become blind." John 9:39, God hear my cry and open my eyes, let me testimony be that You are good, and Your power only gave me sight to see Your will for my life. but whenever a person turns to the Lord, the veil is taken away. Thank You, Lord for the Healed Eyes.

2 Corinthians 3:16 (KJV)

38

The Mother's Prayer

Heavenly Father,

Protect my child from all harm and danger, You, are the Father of

Glory, and all glory belongs to You, God that sees all,

You are the God that redeems; You, are the God that strengthens

the weak. Show mercy to my children. I put my trust in You.

By faith, I know that You, will bring them through.

Wherewithal shall a young man cleanse his way? by taking heed

thereto according to thy word. With my whole heart will I seek

thee: O let me not wander from thy, let your spirit not depart from

me nor, take thy spirit from my child. But protect them all the days

of their life. Why you love us so, I will never know, but this one

thing

I do know, is that You loved us so, that you sent Your only begotten son to die on the cross, and we can never repay You.

Thy word have I hid in mine heart, that I might not sin against thee. Blessed art thou, O LORD: teach me thy statutes.

With my lips have I declared all the judgments of thy mouth?

I have rejoiced in the way of thy testimonies, as much as in all riches. I will meditate in thy precepts, and have respect unto thy ways.

I will delight myself in thy statutes: I will not forget thy word.

Deal bountifully with thy servant, and thy children that we may live, and keep Thy Word. Open our eyes, that we may behold wondrous things out of thy law. In Thy Holy name, we receive thy blessings. Amen, and again I say Amen.

Psalms 119:11-18 (KJV)

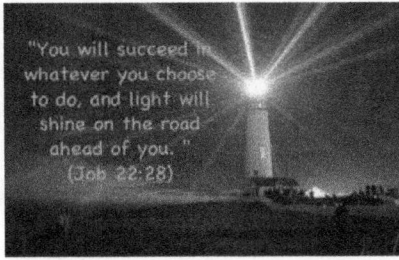

"You will succeed in whatever you choose to do, and light will shine on the road ahead of you. " (Job 22:28)

39

The PM Prayers

Wonderful Counselor,

As I lay my eyes, to rest my soul belongs to You Lord.

I surrender all to You God,

for You are the true and living God.

Let peace sleep by my side,

and mercy and grace embrace me in the morning.

Let no harm come to my door,

nor any sickness befall me. Protect me and my family.

Now when I wake up my Lord,

I will declare that Jesus is Lord, Amen.

THE COAT OF MANY COLORS

40

The Prayer of Many Colors

The Father of Heaven and Earth,

Your created every color there is, for the brightness of Your

creations. I give You Glory and Honor.

Lord Jacob had a favorite son called Joseph,

and he gave him a coat of many colors.

I believe You had a favorite Son call Jesus,

and You gave him the assignment to deliver the world,

on the cross, He finished the work. Today my Lord

I believe Your sons, are called the sons of GOD.

That whosoever may call upon the Lord God, and believe in their

hearts, that Your Son died for our sins, My God,

My Lord, they shall be saved. Joseph had dreams,

The Master's Words for Healing

where his brothers bow down to him. You have given

Your children dreams, as Joseph dreams, came true,

let Your children dreams come true.

As the Lord lives so shall it be, unto the children of God?

Those that walk upright with God, their dreams shall come to pass.

Because You are a God that delivers.

You Delivered back then my God, You, can do it today.

They sold him, as a slave into Egypt,

Let the soul that receives this prayer be free.

Blessed are those that trust in the Lord.

Today My Lord, I claim You as My God,

give me peace and glory, for, in You,

I put my trust, and my hope is not in vain,

Hallelujah, and Amen.

41

The Pre-School Prayer

Dear God,

I love You, For You are my God. Lord, You, are my protector.

Thank You for this day, help me to learn and teach others.

I decree and declare that this is a blessed day.

I will honor and respect others in my school today.

Amen.

42

The Respectable and Honor Prayer

Thy Father of Holiness,

Glory and honor are in his presence; strength and gladness

are in his place. Give unto the Lord, ye kindreds of the people,

give unto the Lord glory and strength.

Give unto the Lord the glory due unto his name: bring an offering,

and come before him: worship the Lord in the beauty of holiness.

My God You are like none other. Peace and Praises belong to

You forever. Thank You for being my God.

Holy, Holy, Holy is the Lord God Almighty.

The One who is, and was, and is to come.

Honor and Glory belong to You forever, Amen.

43

The Spirit of Alcohol

Thy Father of Truth,

Lord let me Walk in Wisdom for Your word says, Be very careful, then, how you live—not as unwise but as wise, making the most of every opportunity, because the days are evil. Therefore, do not be foolish, but understand what the Lord's Will is. Do not get drunk on wine, which leads to debauchery. Instead, be filled with the Spirit, speaking to one another with psalms, hymns, and songs from the Spirit. Sing and make music from your heart to the Lord, always giving thanks to God the Father for everything, in the name of our Lord Jesus Christ. Submit to one another out of reverence for Christ. Spirit of alcohol, I pull down the strong-man hold, that holds me prisoner to alcohol. I plead the blood of Jesus Christ over me and all that I am. Spirit of alcoholism get out of my body, get out of my life; you are no longer welcome here. I am delivered and set free of alcohol from this day forward in Jesus name, Amen.

Ephesians 5: 15-21 (NIV)

44

The Spirit of Autism

Prince of Peace,

I decree and declare that I do not have difficulties

with communication.

I decree, and declare, that socially interactive is normal

to me, and my family.

I speak to the spirit of autism, and

I command you to dry up in the mighty name of Jesus.

I prophesy over my mind, for I have the mind of Christ

Jesus, Lord I know that autism awareness,

can be awesome; but I pray my Lord,

that You heal me from this autism disease.

In Jesus name, Amen.

45

The Spirit of Constipation

The Father of Glory,

All praises belong to You; Thank You for your healing powers my

Lord, I come boldly before the throne of grace, that my prayers

may be answered. Have mercy on me Lord, and heal me from the

inside out. Lord, you are Jehovah Jireh, You, will provide for me;

You are Jehovah Rapha, the great healer, there is none like You.

I destroy the spirit of poverty physically, spiritually, mentally,

and biologically. Lord heaven and earth shall pass away before

Your Word comes back to you void. I bind the spirit of Chronic

Constipation. I plead the blood of Jesus over me,

that I may be made whole. God, You, are the God that heals,

Lord, I know You, as my personal savior. I have not been with

You God, this long for You to forsake me. Satan the Lord rebukes

you concerning me right now loose here;

I terminate your assignment in my life, from this day forward.

I will never be the same, your assignment has been assassinated.

The Master's Words for Healing

I decree and declare, a new season in my life of prophetic

 fulfillment and manifestations to take effect right now.

No weapon formed against me shall prosper, this is my heritage

from the Lord; and my righteousness is from the Lord.

I speak prophetically that I am healed by the blood of the lamb,

saved by grace. I plead the blood of Jesus over me from the top

of my head to the sole of my feet. I take authority in Jesus name;

it is written I am a child of the true living God.

I command this storm to stop, Satan the Lord rebuke you,

you have no power here. The victory is mine,

all power belongs to GOD. I fight back against sickness and pain,

I bind you upon earth, therefore you are bound in heaven,

it is unlawful for you to be here, Get out of my body;

you are evicted. Sickness stop trespassing in the temple of the

Holy Spirit. The Lord is my God and there is healing in his wings.

He shall rescue me. I speak prophetically I command my colon to

function as God has designed. I command every blood pouches,

in my body to dry up the blood of Jesus have been applied.

Grab a Prayer & Hold on Tight

I command waste to release through my bowels normally.

I command all infection to release right now from my body.

I am healed by the Word of the Lord. Lord,

I give You, Honor and Praises for by Your Son's stripes I am

healed. I command all muscles in my body to become strengthened

by the Word of the Lord, there are no spots on my colon.

The oil of joy is flowing through me right now;

I have no pain in this body. I command pressure on my colon to

reduce, my intestinal walls are now becoming thin, and food is

passing through them normally,

I am healed by the Word of the Lord, speak Lord that

I may do Your will. Yes, to Your Will and yes to Your way,

I yield my will, for Your purpose. I decree and declare,

that I have normal bowel movements without a laxative.

My colon is supernaturally widening; my body is now in-line with

the will of God. I command my body, to function in the divine

protocol of God. I bind all abnormal activities in my colon, you must function correctly. I speak prophetically to my colon, muscles, and nerves you are responsible, for packaging and eliminating stool as food moves through the colon, to absorb water while forming stool, and my muscles are supernaturally contracting motions in my colon. I command you to absorb water faster than ever, I command stool to release normally. I command my muscles to supernaturally squeeze to push forward through my rectum. I decree and declare that my nerves and muscles are taking actions now, I decree and declare that I have a normal bowel movement; my body is being strengthened for the glory of the Lord. I decree and declare that the word of God is a CAT scan for my body, whatever it detects it heals. When I speak healing, healing power comes forth in the name of Jesus. I command the pain to stop I high jack you with the word of God. Lord, You, are Jehovah Jireh, you will provide for me. You are Jehovah Nissl my strength; You are Jehovah Shalom my peace.

There is none like You, I seal this prayer in Jesus name, Amen.

This prayer is dedicated to Mrs. Carey Warren. R.I.P. I

46

The Spirit of COPD

Thy Father of Glory,

Thank You that my breathing is normal. I bind up the spirit of COPD. Jesus died for my healing, and by his stripes, I am healed. I decree and declare, then no weapon formed against me shall prosper. and every tongue that rises against me; God is faithful to condemn. I prophesy over my lungs. Today they function the way God created them to. I have enough air in my lungs, to do any activity God has created me to do. My lungs will not prohibit me from doing the assignment that God has on my life.

I command my lungs to be made whole, blood pick up the oxygen to deliver throughout my body in Jesus name Amen.

I decree and declare, today you will function normally.

Holy Spirit breathe on me, in the mighty name of God, the Great I am, the Alpha and the Omega, the Beginning and the End.

COPD I am free from you, my God has healed me in Jesus name, Amen.

47

The Spirit of Deadly STD such as Chlamydia, Gonorrhea, Hepatitis-B

Thy Father of Mercy,

Thank You, Lord, for Your healing power. Thank You, God,

that You're God all by yourself. Spirit of STD.

I command you to dry up right now, in the mighty name of Jesus.

Spirit of STD you have no power over my life, for I am a child of

the Most High God. Jesus Christ took the sting out of infirmity,

and death all power belongs to God. I come in the volume of the

Holy Bible, and in the power, of Jesus Christ. Spirit STD,

Chlamydia, Gonorrhea and Hepatitis B dry up, Dry up in the name

of Jesus. I decree and declare, that the word of God is a CAT scan

for my body, whatever it detects the word of God heals.

Thank You, God, for my healing, Amen.

48

The Spirit of Diabetes

O' Mighty God,

Teach me Your will that I may follow, guide my steps,

into the right path; for Your Word says. The steps of a good man,

is ordered by the Lord. Order my steps, my Lord that I may follow

You, all the days of my life. For I will declare, the healing of the

Lord, that You have done a great thing, and mankind will know,

that You are my God. You are my healer, You, are my Savior,

and no other gods will I serve. For I Thank You, for healing me of

diabetes. I thank You, for changing the red blood cells, to the way

You call them to be. When You created Adam. I Thank You, my

God, that my white blood cells are becoming normal, cooperating

and function the way You form them in the days of old. Diabetes

get out of my body in Jesus name. Hallelujah to Your Holy name.

I give You honor glory and praises. I'm Healed of diabetes in the

Mighty name of Jesus, Amen. Hallelujah and Amen, Lord I love

You have Your way today in my life; my trust is in You Lord, Amen.

49

The Spirit of Disorderly Behavior

Thy Father of Truth,

Your word says, You, would keep my mind in perfect peace. Disorderly behavior, I bind you up, and destroy the root of disorderly behavior; I am made whole in Jesus name. I command my mind, to represent Christ in the Earthly Realm. Our Father which art in heaven, Hallowed be thy name, the kingdom come, thy will be done, as it is in heaven. Give us this day, Our Daily Bread, and forgive us our debts, as we forgive our debtors and lead us not into temptation; but Deliver Us from evil, for thine is the kingdom and the power, and the glory, forever amen. Matthew 6:9-13 For we hear that there are some, which walk among you disorderly, working not at all, but are busybodies. Lord let me forever keep a blameless heart, let me forever walk upright with mankind and You my Lord. For my trust is in the Lord, Amen.

Matthew 6:9-13, 2 Thessalonians 3 (KJV)

50

The Spirit of Down-Syndrome

Thy Father of Holiness,

My Lord, You, make no mistakes, for I am made in Your image,

and when You made mankind Your word says. So, God,

created man in His own image, in the image of God, created he

him, male and female created he them. Thank You for creating me,

Thank You for healing me, Thank You for saving me,

Thank You, God, for delivering me in the time of need.

I count this down syndrome a privilege, because many can't

carry this disease; but You will put no more on me,

than I can bear through Christ Jesus. I can do all things because

You are the one that strengthens me, Lord. For this day,

I choose to receive Your healing of this down syndrome,

and I Thank You in advance, for Your Miracles Your Signed,

and Your Wonders in the land of the living. Heal Me Lord and

The Master's Words for Healing

I will be careful to give You the honor, the glory, and the Praises.

which You so rightfully deserve, in Jesus Mighty name, Amen.

I seal this prayer in heaven and therefore it's sealed in the earth

I am healed.

51

The Spirit of Drug Addiction

Wonderful Counselor,

Stop the drugs from calling my name, this spirit of drug addiction has taken so much out of my life. I allowed the drugs to control me, to manipulate my mind. I destroy the spirit of drug addiction, in the power and name of Jesus. Get out of my body, get out of my life. Your assignment is terminated in my life, God is in control. God, I know You have not forsaken me, for You will deliver me, from this drug addiction, physically, mentally, and biologically. Lord Your word cannot come back to You void. I bind the spirit of drug addiction, I plead the blood of Jesus, over my mind, body, and soul. I am set free of this addiction. Lord, forgive me of all my sins. Show me how to forgive others. That I may be forgiven and set free. I take a leap of faith and I forgive anyone that has wronged me. Lord take away this addiction, that I may serve You to the fullest all the days of my life. Satan, I serve you notice that I

The Master's Words for Healing

am free from this drug addiction, You, no longer control my life,

but from this day forward I claim victory over this drug addiction,

 I decree and declare, that I no longer have the taste

of drugs in my mouth.

I am no longer, feening fiend for a fix. I crave God.

I decree and declare, that my mind and body function,

as if I had never had this drug in my system.

For today and every day, I choose to be, Drug-Free,

Amen.

52

The Spirit of Shingles

Thy Father of Love,

Thank You, for creating heaven and earth, Thank You,

for Your Precious Son blood; for by His stripes I am healed,

But He was wounded for our transgressions, He was bruised

for our iniquity, the chastisement of our peace was upon Him

and with His stripes, we are healed. I come in the power of God,

and in the volume of His Holy book, through the authority of Jesus

Christ. This Chicken Pox virus that is causing painful rashes.

I command the pain to stop in the Mighty name of Jesus.

I lay my hands on my head and decree, and declare,

that my body is being made whole through the blood,

and the power of Jesus Christ. Spirit of shingles dry up,

and vanish right now, in the Mighty name of Jesus.

You are no longer welcome in my body get out.

God let this be as Your Words are true.

The Master's Words for Healing

'Take My yoke upon you and learn from Me, for I am gentle and humble in heart, and YOU WILL FIND REST FOR YOUR SOULS. For My yoke is easy and My burden is light. Thank You, Lord, for healing me, Amen.

Isaiah 53 5, Matthew 11: 29-30

PRAYER / FAITH

53

The Spirit of Faith

Yes Lord,

I Thank You for my faith, Your power and Your glory in my life.
I have not hid thy righteousness within my heart; I have declared
thy faithfulness and thy salvation: I have not concealed thy
lovingkindness and thy truth from the great congregation.
Therefore, I know that You are great, O Lord God. For there is
none like You, nor is there any God besides You, according to all
that we have heard with our ears, or seen with our eyes. There is no
wrong in You. You sit high and look low. You are God all by
Yourself. For that I thank You. Increase my faith and strengthen
me, to endure the test that will build my faith. In Jesus Mighty
name, I pray this prayer, Amen.

Psalms 40:10, 2 Samuel 7:22 (KJV)

54

The Spirit of Gambling

How Excellent is thy Name,

The God that created heaven and earth have mercy on me,

for I need Your help today. This spirit of gambling has captured

me and I am a slave to it, for when I do not want to gamble the

spirit calls me to engage in gambling activities.

I neglect my responsibilities, I have forgotten my first love which

is You, my Lord. All things are lawful unto me,

but all things are not expedient: all things are lawful for me,

but I will not be brought under the power of any.

Gambling spirit you have no power over me anymore.

For God has given me the liberty to worship Him in Spirit and in

truth. But if any provide not for his own, and especially for those

of his own house, he have denied the faith and is worse than an

infidel. Teach me, Lord, to do Your will and deliver me from this

spirit of gambling. God show me a better way to survive, for I

know this is not Your will for my life.

I bind the spirit of gambling, in my mind, body, and soul,

therefore, I am set free of gambling.

I am free to give God the Glory, Amen.

1 Corinthians 6:12, 1 Timothy 5:8 (KJV)

55

The Spirit of Gout

Everlasting Father,

Blessed is the man Who walks not in the counsel of the ungodly, nor stands in the path of sinners, nor sits in the seat of the scornful, But his delight is in the law of the Lord, And in His law, he meditates day and night. He shall be like a tree Planted by the rivers of water, that brings forth its fruit in its season, whose leaf also shall not wither; And whatever he does shall prosper. The ungodly are not so, but are like the chaff which the wind drives away. Therefore, the ungodly shall not stand in the judgment, Nor sinners in the congregation of the righteous. For the Lord knows the way of the righteous, But the way of the ungodly shall perish. Lord heal me, of this spirit of gout, that I may move freely to praise You all the days of my life, Amen.

Psalm 1-9 (KJV)

56

The Spirit of Guilt and Shame

Thy Father of Peace,

You are my great shame destroyer, there is none like You.

I decree and declare that I am set free through the sanctification

of Jesus Christ, who died on the cross for all my sins.

I come in the name of Jesus have mercy on me. Let not shame or

guilt dwell in my heart. Let me not be coved with grief.

My Lord, You, have forgiven me of all my sins, You,

have created in me a clean heart. You have renewed a right spirit.

My flesh fights against me, day and night tormenting me

with guilt and shame. I speak the words to forgive myself.

I take responsibilities for my own actions.

I no longer live by the flesh but my members are directed by the

spirit of the Lord. Gen. 4:7 says "If you do well, will you not be

accepted? And if you do not do well, sin lies at the door.

And its desire is for you, but you should rule over it."

Teach me Holy Spirit to never be ashamed for my Father

is in heaven who loves me so. Ex.9:27 say's

"And Pharaoh sent and called for Moses and Aaron,

and said to them," "I have sinned this time.

The Lord is righteous, and my people and I are wicked."

I take up the will of the Lord from this day forth

I will never be the same. Satan the Lord rebukes you

concerning me this day; guilt and shame loose here forever more,

thank you, Lord, for taking it all away. Ezr. 9:6 say's

"And I said: "O my Lord, I am too ashamed and humiliated to

lift up my face to You, my God; our iniquities have risen higher

than our heads, and our guilt has grown up to the heavens."

Then I reminded the Lord of His words,

I am a child of the Living God, saved by grace and forgiven

of all my sin. And the Lord heard my cry, He rescued me in the

time of trouble. For I look to the hills,

from which cometh my help, my help comes from the Lord.

In Jesus name, I seal this prayer, Amen.   Ezra. 9:6, Exodus 9:27 (KJV)

57

The Spirit of Headaches

How Excellent is thy Name,

I plead the blood of Jesus over me, from the top of my head to the sole of my feet; that I may be made whole in Jesus name.

I lay my hand, on my head, and command this headache to be gone. Pain dry up in the Mighty name of Jesus.

I speak prophetically over my body that my body is made whole by the word and the power of God.

I am healed in Jesus name, Amen.

58

The Spirit of HIV/AIDS

Thy Father of Love,

God, I thank You, that You are a good God. Praise the Lord, my soul; all that is within me, praise His Holy name. Praise the Lord, my soul, and forget not all his benefits, Who, forgives all your sins, and heals all your diseases, Who, redeems your life, from the pit, and crowns you with love, and compassion, who satisfies your desires with good things, so that your youth is renewed like the eagle's. Heal me Lord of Human Immunodeficiency Virus, and Acquired Immune Deficiency Syndrome. I decree, and declare, that my immune system is becoming normal and there are no syndromes of HIV or AIDS, in Jesus name, Amen. O Lord, create in me a clean heart, O God; and renew a right spirit within me. But He was wounded for our transgressions,

He was bruised for our iniquities: the chastisement of our peace was upon him, and with His stripes, we are healed.

Psalms 103:1-5, Psalms 51:10, Isaiah 53:5 (KJV)

Holiness
TO THE
Lord

59

The Spirit of Holiness

Thy Father of Holiness,

You, my God, Are Holy, therefore I am Holy; because your spirit

lives in me. I prayed for a fresh anointing of holiness to fall fresh

on me. Thy Father of Peace I pray for clarity my God,

fresh anointing fall on me. Favor arrive at my doorstep,

Let healing hold me up on my right and left side.

Provision meet me at the door. that I may declare the word of God.

I govern my house with God Direction. I walk up right before man

and I turn from evil. Having therefore, these promises,

Dearly beloved, let us cleanse ourselves from all filthiness of the

flesh and spirit, perfecting holiness in the fear of God.

2 Corinthians 7:1, I will Follow peace with all men, and holiness,

without which no man shall see the Lord: Hebrews 12:14

The Master's Words for Healing

In the mighty name of Jesus,

I declare and decree that this prayer become law, in the land of the

living, and in heaven, Amen.

60

The Spirit of Homosexuality

Heavenly Father,

I come to You my God today trusting and believe that You

are God and that You can make me whole. You, my God,

can make a way out of no way.

I come in the volume of the Holy Bible, set me free

that I may worship You in spirit and in truth.

Regardless of how I got these feelings or how I became this way.

God, I trust You that Your words cannot come back to You void.

So today I am standing on Your Words, and I am casting all my

cares upon You my God. For I know that You care for me.

Deliver me O'Lord in the mighty name of Jesus.

Heal me of this homosexuality. I bind up the thoughts, the

activities and any residue of this homosexuality spirit.

I take authority in the power of God and in the name of Jesus.

Spirit of homosexuality I cancel every assignment and arrest any

activities in my life concerning all homosexuality deeds.

The Master's Words for Healing

I loose the spirit of liberty and the power of God in my life today,

In Jesus name. I know that Your word says,

For God so loved the world, that he gave his only begotten Son,

that whosoever believeth in him should not perish,

but have everlasting life. God whatever is in me that is not pleasing

to you, heal me and show me that I may make it right with You.

God, I ask You to forgive me of all my sins, blot out my

transgressions and deliver me. For the grace of God has appeared,

bringing salvation to all men, instructing us to deny ungodliness

and worldly desires and to live sensibly, righteously and godly in

the present age, Therefore I run in such a way, as not without aim;

I box in such a way, as not beating the air; but I discipline my body

and make it my slave, so that after I have preached to others,

I myself will not be disqualified. To testify of the Lord's goodness

for by Grace we are Saved, Amen.

John 3:16, Titus 2:11-12, 1 Corinthians 9:26-27 (KJV)

Special Notes! To my friends, and them that choose,

to live in Homosexuality. let it be between you and God,

for grace is given to all mankind. But unto them,

that wants to be Free of this spirit. May the Lord free you,

and may you stay free, all the days of your life. Godspeed.

61

The Spirit of Hypertension

Thy Father of Righteousness,

You are my great healer, I decree and declare, that the beta

blockers are slowing the heart rate down. God reduce how hard;

my heart should work. I bind the spirit of hypertension; therefore,

you are now inactive, through the blood, and power of Jesus

Christ. My body is becoming normal in the powers of the Holy

Spirit, that flows through me, and my body through salvation.

Heavenly Father, if I am smoking, becoming overweight, little

physical activities, too much salt intake in my body. Or if I have

consumed too much alcohol give me the power and the strength to

become whole in Jesus mighty name. Now, Lord, Your Word says;

But unto you, that fear my name, shall the Son of righteousness

arise with healing in His wings, and ye shall go forth and grow up,

as calves of the stall. Blessed be the name of the Lord. Bless the

Lord, O My soul: and all that is within me, bless His Holy name.

I pull down all strongholds in my life. For the glory of God is my reward in Jesus holy name, Amen.

Malachi 4:2, Psalms 103:3, Isaiah 58:8 (KJV)

62

The Spirit of Sleep Disorder

Thy Father of Truth,

I bind up, any sleep deprivation in my life, I speak prophetically in the Word and Power of God. That every sleep disorder,

in my body has been executed in my life, and my sleeping habits are normal, in Jesus name Amen.

I decree and declare that I have no problems with high blood pressure or heart disease and no stroke symptoms. Now Lord

So that I come again to my father's house in peace; then shall the LORD be my God: and I shall sleep in peace.

For you will keep in perfect peace those whose minds are steadfast because they trust in you. I trust You, Lord, to heal me of this sleeping disorder, and I receive my healing in Jesus name, Amen.

Genesis 28:21, Isaiah 26:3 (KJV)

63

The Spirit of Suicide

Thy Father of Love and Peace,

Have mercy, on me for I have sinned against You my God

Finally, my brethren, be strong in the Lord,

and in the power of his might. For though we walk in the flesh,

we do not war after the flesh: Satan I serve you notice on earth,

and it's footnoted in heaven.

You have no power over me.

The Lord rebukes you concerning me. Get out of my life.

I will do good from this day forward.

For the weapons of our warfare are not carnal,

but mighty through God to the pulling down of strongholds;

Casting down imaginations, and every high thing that exalt

itself against the knowledge of God, and bringing into

captivity every thought to the obedience of Christ;

I will not reduce myself to suicide for God loves me.

Put on the whole armor of God, that you may be able to stand

against the wiles of the devil. For we wrestle not against flesh

and blood, but against principalities, against powers,

against the rulers of the darkness of this world, against spiritual

wickedness in high places. Wherefore take unto you the whole

armor of God, that you may be able to withstand in the evil day,

and having done all, to stand.

Stand therefore, having your loins girt about with truth, and having

on the breastplate of righteousness; And your feet shod with the

preparation of the gospel of peace; Above all, taking the shield of

faith, wherewith ye shall be able to quench all the fiery darts of the

wicked. And take the helmet of salvation, and the sword of the

Spirit, which is the word of God: Spirit of suicide you lose,

For my life belongs to God, Amen.

Ephesians 6:10-17, 2 Corinthians 10:5

64

The Spirit of Loneliness

Thy Father of Glory,

God thank You for not leaving me, nor forsaking me.

I will Trust in the Lord, and do good; I will Dwell in the land, and

feed on His faithfulness. Be strong and of good courage,

do not fear nor be afraid of them; for the Lord your God,

He is the One who goes with you. He will not leave you nor

forsake you." When my father and my mother forsake me,

Then the Lord will take care of me.

And I heard a great voice out of heaven saying,

Behold, the tabernacle of God is with men, and he will dwell with

them, and they shall be his people, and God himself shall be with

them, and be their God, Amen. Spirit of loneliness, my joy is from

the Lord. Loneliness is gone, I am happy in the Lord, Amen.

Psalms 37:3, Psalms 27:10, Deuteronomy 31:6, Revelations 21:3 (KJV)

65

The Spirit of Love

Thy Father of Love,

God, Your Everlasting Love is always with me.

Thank You for loving me even when I was not fit to be loved.

Thank You for sending Your Son to die on Calvary so many

years ago. He died for me when I wasn't lovable.

But Your Word God changes things and today

I feel Your love for me. That I am alive, and not dead.

Thank You for Life. For Your mercy and Your grace.

Lord, I love You. Because You are God all by Yourself.

What then shall we say to these things? God is for us,

who can be against us? He who did not spare His Own Son,

but delivered Him up for us all, how shall He not with Him

also freely give us all things? Who shall bring a charge against

God's elect? It is God who justifies.   Romans 8:31-33 (KJV)

66

The Spirit of Lupus Erythematous

O Mighty God,

How I love to praise Your name, Holy, Holy.

Is the Lord God Almighty, The one who is, and is to come,

I bind up all pain from Lupus. I command the pain to dry up

and cease. My labor is not in vain. The presence of the Lord is

here. I feel like praising the Lord for I know that You, my God,

is great, all that You do, My God is good.

Thank You, Lord, for your grace and Your mercy.

Give me the power to kill this sickness in my life.

God your words give life and death.

Now I take authority in Jesus mighty name.

I decree and declare that I have no inflammatory disease in my

body, and my immune system will never again attack its own

tissues.

now my Lord, by the blood of Jesus Christ I am healed. Hallelujah

and, Amen.

67

The Spirit of Masturbation

Thy Father of Glory,

Have mercy on me O Lord, for my sins are before You,

hear a just calls, hide not your face from me,

but my lord turn Your ear to my call. For my sins have consumed

me, and lust have corrupted me, what must I do to be delivered;

there is no one, that can rescue me but God.

 I lift my hands up, to Your Holy throne as Your Word says.

Spirit of Hedonism, you are a demonic sexual stronghold.

I Cast you down, and out of my mind, body, and soul.

Now the works of the flesh are manifest, which are these;

Adultery, fornication, uncleanness, lasciviousness,

Let the redeemed, of the Lord, say so; Now my Lord,

If You say I am delivered of the spirit of masturbation

it shall be so if they will learn carefully,

the ways of My people, to swear by My name,

'As the LORD lives,'

The Master's Words for Healing

as they taught, my people to swear by Baal,

then they shall be established,

in the midst of My people. From this day forward,

I decree and declare, that I am not ignorant of this issue,

surrounding the spirit of masturbation.

I take on the mind of Jesus Christ.

The wisdom and intellect. Today I move forward to

my reality and understanding that there are consequences

of my actions. I rebuke the spirit of lust,

and Hedonism off my body. Now Satan, loose me,

and let me go, in the Mighty name of Jesus;

unclean spirit loose me now. In the power of God,

I am free from masturbation's spirit in Jesus name Amen.

Stay free, because it will take over your flesh,

and the devil will be in control again.

You will have guilt and condemnation and

The Lord wants you to be FREE!

Galatians 5:19, Jeremiah 12:16 (KJV)

68

The Spirit of Mental Imbalance

Thy Father of Peace,

I proclaim, that there is no mental imbalance,

such as depression, anxiety, or bipolar in my DNA.

For God has given me the mind of Christ,

that I may worship Him in Spirit and in truth.

The bible says and always, night and day,

he was in the mountains, and in the tombs, crying,

and cutting himself with stones. But when he saw Jesus afar off,

he ran and worshipped Him, and cried with a loud voice,

and said, what have I to do with thee,

Jesus, thou Son of the most high God? I adjure thee by God,

that thou torment me not. For he said unto him,

Come out of the man, thou unclean spirit.

Now my God if an unclean spirit worshipped You,

give me a clear mind to worship You in Spirit and in truth.

That I may know that You are my God, Amen.   Mark 5:5-8 (KJV)

69

The Spirit of Parkinson

Thy Father of Holiness,

Enter into his gates with thanksgiving, and into his courts with

praise: be thankful unto him, and bless his name.

Lord stop the tremoring in my hands, take away the slow

movement and stiffness. And he said unto me,

my grace is sufficient for thee: for my strength is made perfect

in weakness. Most gladly, therefore, will I rather glory in my

infirmities, that the power of Christ may rest upon me.

Then I shall know in my heart that I shall serve the

LORD my God, and he shall bless thy bread, and thy water;

and my God said I will take sickness away from the midst of thee.

Now, my God, I will worship you all the days of my life,

Amen.

Psalm 100:4, 2 Corinthians 12:9, Exodus 23:25 (KJV)

70

The Spirit of Polio

Thy Father of Righteousness,

I decree, and declare, that any development of paralysis

is drying up in my body right now.

Holy Spirit speak to me,

that I may know the true and living God.

And Jesus went about all Galilee, teaching in their synagogues,

and preaching the gospel of the kingdom, and healing,

all manner of sickness, and all manner of disease,

among the people. Thank You, God, Your,

healing power is still alive and active in the land of the living.

Amen. I receive my complete healing from polio in Jesus name,

Amen.

Matthew 4:23 (KJV)

71

The Spirit of Pornography

Thy Father of Mercy,

Have mercy on me, for I have let this spirit of pornography

get the best of me. My sexual appetite is not the one

that you created me to have. When You said let there be light, let

Your light shine in my life all the days of my life.

This spirit entices me to interact with unclean spirits

when I want to do right. The pornography spirit calls me

to do things, that are not pleasing to you my God.

Show me how not to answer to the unclean spirit.

Deliver and Save me from this spirit of pornography.

And there was in their synagogue a man with an unclean spirit,

and he cried out, O' my Lord, hear my cry, hide not Your face

from me, but help me God I pray. Spirit of pornography,

I bind you up in Jesus name, get out of my mind, body,

and soul; I belong to God. Thank You, Lord. Amen.

Mark 1:23 (KJV)

72

The Spirit of Prostate

Thy Father of Grace,

Lord, I proclaim that it is You my God that will bless me.

And when he had called unto him his twelve disciples,

He gave them power against unclean spirits, to cast them out,

and to heal all manner of sickness and all manner of disease.

My God For by thee I have run through a troop,

and by my God have I leaped over a wall. As for God,

His way is perfect: the word of the Lord is tried:

He is a buckler to all those that trust in Him. I decree and declare

that the shaking stops now. my Lord I pray that You heal me from

Prostate that I may be whole in Jesus name.

God, I trust in You. Thank You for healing me, Amen.

Matthew 10:1, Psalm 18:29-30 (KJV)

73

Thy Spirit of Rheumatoid Arthritis

Heavenly Father,

Dry up the chronic inflammatory disorder,

affecting many of my joints. That I may praise You

in spirit and in truth.

My God the doctors say that this condition can't be cured.

but I know a doctor, name Jesus; that can heal all diseases.

He can calm the water in the storm. He can raise the dead.

Surely My God can heal me.

I decree and declare that the arthritis is drying up in my body,

and my body is becoming whole.

For the testimonies of the saints. Then we shall know;

That it might be fulfilled which was spoken by Esaias

the prophet, saying, Himself took our infirmities,

and bare our sicknesses. Thank You, God, for healing me.

Amen.   Matthew 8:17 (KJV)

74

The Spirit of Shopaholic

Wonderful Counselor,

Shopping is ruining my life. Lord, it did not start out like this,

but now I have no control over it.

When I go into the stores, I often get my God

what I don't even need. Teach me, Lord,

the things that I need, and show me the things that I want

is not accentual to my life. Feel the void that's inside me;

that gives me satisfaction from shopping.

You are my God deliver me from this shopaholic.

I declare that I will not buy what I do not need.

Help me Lord, to stop shopping unnecessarily.

I claim healing in the Mighty Name of Jesus, Amen.

75

The Spirit of Shoplifting

Thy Father of Truth,

God, You, are awesome, You, are righteous.

God everything You do is good. Lord,

I come before you, as humble as I know how.

I keep stealing things from the smallest to the largest.

Forgive me God and deliver me Lord

from this shoplifting spirits. I need Your Help, Lord.

I decree and decree that this shoplifting spirit is being terminated

in my life. I arrest the spirit of shoplifting. For the Bible says,

that the enemy comes to steal kill and destroy.

That's not my future, and I bind up every demonic spirit

that has tempted me to steal. I execute the spirit of lying in my life.

I terminate the spirit of deception in my life.

For God has delivered me, I received my Deliverance

in Jesus, Mighty name. I am set free and who the son sets free

is free indeed. Hallelujah, Thank You, Lord, Amen.

76

The Spirit of the Compulsive Lying

Thy Father of Peace,

Lord forgive me, for this compulsive lying spirit.

Your Word says and the chief priests and all the council

sought for witness, against Jesus to put him to death;

and found none. For many bare false witnesses against him,

but their witness agreed not together. Lord,

I have got caught up in my lies, I have caused harmful accusations,

and confusion, in so many people lives. I have told so many lies,

that I have confused myself, between the truth and a lie,

forgive me, God. I cancel every demonic assignment on my life.

I break the lying tongue in my mouth; with the word of God,

from this day forward. God only allow me, to speak the truth,

regardless of the consequences.

In Jesus Mighty name, Amen.

77

The Spirit of the Creutzfeldt Jakob Diseases

Heavenly Father,

I have heard the doctor report,

concerning the Creutzfeldt Jakob Diseases.

They say it is an incurable, and universally.

 Fatal neurodegenerative disease,

My God they even called it the mad cow disease.

Now, my God, I know that You are a Healing God.

You are my Lord and King. There is none like You.

As for God, His way is perfect; the word of the LORD is tried:

He is a buckler, to all them that trust in Him.

Lord, I am trusting in You. I receive my healing right now. Thank

You, Lord. When Jesus heard that, He said,

this sickness is not unto death, but for the glory of God,

that the Son of God might be glorified thereby.

Be glorified my God, forever and ever, Amen.

John 11:4 (KJV)

78

The Spirit of Tobacco

Thy Father of Glory,

Heavenly Father, help me. Let smoking not be my demise.

Empower me to stop smoking in Jesus name I pray,

all things are possible, to them that believe,

Lord, I believe that You can help me thank You,

Lord. I am delivered from smoking, Satan you don't win;

my victory is in Jesus. Amen. Jehovah Machsi, the Lord

is my refuge, peace be unto You. Lord, there are more deaths,

caused by tobacco use than, by all deaths from humans.

Rescue me for I need Your help. I have tried doing this on

my own, but I have failed. Knowing that my failures,

in tobacco use is not my destiny.

"Smoking causes an estimated 90% of all lung cancer,

deaths in men and 80% of all lung cancer deaths in women.

An estimated 90% of all deaths from chronic obstructive lung

disease are caused by smoking. www.cdc.gov/tobacco."

Lord let me not be in these numbers in Jesus name, Amen.

79

The Spirit of Warfare in the Time of Need

Thy Father of Glory,

Thank You, Lord, for Your grace and Your mercy that endures

forever. My God You said Beware of false prophets, which come

to you in sheep's clothing, but inwardly they are ravening wolves.

And I know my Lord that we wrestle not against flesh and blood,

but against principalities, against powers, against the rulers of the

darkness of this world, against spiritual wickedness in high places.

Wherefore take unto you the whole armour of God, that ye may

be able to withstand in the evil day, and having done all, to stand.

I cancel every Demonic spirit of warfare, that has come against me

and my family through the blood of Jesus Christ. Spirit of warfare

you are decapitated, get out of my life from this day forward you

are beaten.   Ephesians 6:12-13, Matthew 7:15

(KJV)

80

The Teenage Prayer

Thy Father of Righteousness,

Show me how to make good decisions,

that I may choose to do great things.

Empower me, Lord, to understand quicker.

Equip me to complete assignments simpler.

Protect me Lord, all the days of my life.

Remember not the sins of my youth, nor my transgressions:

according to thy mercy, remember thou me for thy goodness'

sake, O LORD. For thou art my hope, O Lord GOD:

thou art my trust from my youth. Hallelujah, God,

I trust in You keep me in perfect peace Amen.

Psalms 25:7, Psalms 71:5 (KJV)

81

Un-forgiveness and Resentment

Thy Father of Peace,

Give ear to my prayer O God, hide not Your face from me.

Incline Your ear to my call. My Lord My God

 sin has kept me from your presence. For it is me

O Lord and not my enemy, who approaches me,

un-forgiveness and resentment grip my heart.

Show me how to forgive, that I may be forgiven.

For I am not ashamed of the gospel of Christ:

for it is the power of God, unto salvation to every one

that believeth; to the Jew first, and also to the Greek.

For therein is the righteousness of God, revealed from faith

to faith: as it is written, the just shall live by faith.

Now, my Lord, I release all un-forgiveness and

resentment in my heart, and take up the Spirit of Christ,

to live in peace, Amen.

Prayers That Strengthen Your Faith

82

A Blameless Heart

Thy Father of Truth,

Show me, God, how to live holy, (Qadosh).

That my life actions reflect Your characters.

Worship the Lord in the beauty of holiness.

That ye may be blameless and harmless, the sons of God,

without rebuke, in the midst of a crooked and perverse

nation, among whom ye shine as lights in the world;

And the very God of peace sanctify you wholly,

and I pray God your whole spirit and soul and body

be preserved blameless unto the coming of

our Lord Jesus Christ.

Philippians 2:15, 1 Thessalonians 5:23 (KJV)

83

A Right Decision

Thy Father of Peace,

There are Multitudes, multitudes of decisions

in the valley of decision: for the day of the LORD

is near in the valley of decision.

I take authority over confusion, I disallow and annihilate

any confusion, chaos, and frustration upon me for making

the right decision. for my situation at hand. I thank You,

Lord in advance for Your Miracles, Your Signs, and Your

Wonders. for they follow the gospel, and I decree that

You are Lord of lords, and my God You are King of Kings.

Therefore, I declare there is no God None Like You.

For You Are the Great I Am, the Alpha and the Omega,

the Beginning and the End.

Thank You, Lord for Your grace and Your mercy

in Jesus mighty name, Amen.

Joel 3:14 (KJV)

84

Braking the Spirit of Un-forgiveness

Thy Father of Truth,

The LORD is longsuffering, and of great mercy, forgiving iniquity and transgression, and by no means clearing the guilty, visiting the iniquity of the fathers upon the children, unto the third and fourth generation. Thank You, Lord, for forgiving me, I brake the spirit of un-forgiveness through the blood of Jesus Christ.

For I put my trust in God. For the word says, and be ye kind one to another, tenderhearted, forgiving one another, even as God for Christ's sake hath forgiven you. Because of God's forgiveness, I possess the power of forgiveness and forgive all that have harmed me and my family. I Plead the blood of Jesus Christ, over me and all that I love, Amen.

Numbers 14:18, Ephesians 4:32 (KJV)

85

Breaking Soul Ties to Darkness

Thy Father of Righteousness,

God, You, are infinite, and there is no wrong in You. My God,

You, are my Jehovah-M'Kaddesh. You have forgiven

me and sanctified me, that I may stand in power and glory.

I take authority in the name of Jesus. I decree and declare that

I break all soul ties, to the kingdom of darkness.

And releasing the spirit of liberty. That I may worship God

in spirit and truth. I repent of all sins, and ask God to forgive me;

I forgive anyone that has sin against me. Braking all soul

ties to darkness in the Mighty name of Jesus. For I know,

He will keep the feet of his saints, and the wicked shall be

silent in darkness; for by strength shall no man prevail,

Amen.

1 Samuel 2:9 (KJV)

86

Emotional Damage Deliverance

Wonderful Counselor,

Thou art my King, O God: command deliverances for Jacob.

And me my Lord. Command all emotional damages concerning

me, to be terminated for the peace of my mind. I claim Deliverance

in Jesus name. For I put my trust in You Lord. Thou art my hiding

place; thou shalt preserve me from trouble; thou shalt compass me

about with songs of deliverance. Selah. You are Jehovah- Jireh,

You, have and always will provide for me, fresh anointing let

deliverance fall upon me, my God is Elohim, He gives me strength

and power to rise above all that the enemy has sent my way, today

I shall receive power and peace because of Jehovah Shalom,

is my peace. To God be the glory, Amen.

Psalms 44:4, Psalms 32:7 (KJV)

87

Favor in the Work Place

Heavenly Father,

I am walking in victory, I am walking in peace with God,

favor is in this place, favor is upon my life.

I am walking in holiness I am walking in righteousness;

for I trust in God to give me favor in my work place,

empower me, my God to be effective today in this place.

For all power and glory belongs to God.

I will commit my work to the Lord, and then your plans

will succeed, Therefore, my beloved be steadfast, immovable,

always excelling in the work of the Lord, because you know that

in the Lord, your labor is not in vain.

Proverbs 16:3, 1 Corinthians (KJV)

88

Frustrating the Enemy

Thy Father of Peace,

Lord, I trust You, to protect me against the enemy,

for You are my God, and through You my God,

all things are possible to them that believe.

No weapon formed against me shall prosper and every

tongue that rises against me. You, my God will condemn.

Every trap that the enemy, has set for me,

is now being uprooted in the soil of conception,

and it will never prevail.

I command darkness to overtake my enemies.

I command drought and confusion to overshadow them.

Dismiss all assignments my enemies have for me and my family.

in Jesus name, Amen.

89

Heavens Instructions

Thy Father of Glory,

I now know, when God speaks it's not a suggestion,

it's a direction. If you're looking for heaven instruction,

then all you should do is get on your knees and cry out to God.

Ask God, what shall I do about my life,

God, how do I lead my children, and family.

God show me unique way to handle my job.

What shall I do about this situation at hand.

Lord You created me to behold the beauty of Your Works.

Now, Lord, I need heavens instruction, in my life today.

I must fully understand clearly the Words You speak to my soul.

Give me Your instructions my Lord and I will not waver with them.

In the Mighty name of Jesus, Amen.

90

Peace in the Valley of Decision's

Thy Father of Victory,

Settle it therefore in your heart, not to meditate before what ye shall answer: For I will give you, a mouth and wisdom, which all your adversaries shall not be able to gainsay, nor resist.

Be clear in your heart, and know that the Lord your God, will give you what you need, in the time of decision. I will not lean to my own understanding but in all my ways. I will acknowledge You. My God, for the decision that I must make. I trust and believe, that You, my God, will lead me into the right decision.

For You, O Lord created heaven and earth. Now, my Lord, I'm going to follow You, all the days of my life. and in this Valley of the decision, I will do according to Your Will, and Your Way.

For I know, You, have already worked this out, for my good.

I trust, and believe in Your Holy Word, in Jesus name, Amen.

Luke 21:14-15 (KJV)

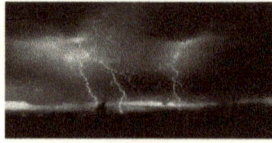

91

Praying through the Storms

Prince of Peace,

I am going to, pray my way through this storm Lord,

I am Praying through the storm. Guide my feet Lord that

I may see all that enemy has laid before me.

Stop my enemies in their tracks, that no harm or destruction

come to my doors. Guide my feet, Lord, that I may not stumble.

Show me the way that You would have me to go.

Because I choose You to be my God and no other God

I choose to serve, but You are Alpha and Omega,

You are the Beginning and the End. With You all things are

possible, but without You nothing is possible.

so, I'm standing firm, during this storm. trusting and believing in Your Holy Word. You are my God, You, are my banner, and

You are my Shield. You will not cause me to stumble nor fall, but

You will uphold me with Your righteousness.

and I Will Rise Above This Storm and super exceed all that

You have for me to do Lord, Amen.

92

Praying with the names of God in your daily prayers

Jehovah my GOD – Ask Jehovah to empower your daily prayer life.

Jehovah – The Lord Exodus 6:2, 3

Adonai Jehovah – The Lord God Genesis 15:2

Jehovah Adon Kal Ha'arets –the Lord of All the Earth Joshua 3:11

Jehovah Bara – The Lord Creator Isaiah 40:28

Jehovah Chezeq – The Lord My Strength Psalm 18:1

Jehovah Chereb – The Lord. the Sword Deut. 33:29

Jehovah Eli – The Lord My God Psalm 18:2

Jehovah Ely on – The Lord Most High Genesis 14:18

Jehovah 'Ez-Lami – The Lord My Strength Psalm 28:7

Jehovah Gador Milchamah – The Lord Mighty in Battle Psalm 24:8

Jehovah Ganan – The Lord Our Defense Psalm 89:18

Jehovah Go'el – The Lord Thy Redeemer Isaiah 49:26; 60:16

Jehovah Hashopet – The Lord the Judge Judges 11:27

Jehovah Hoshe'ah – The Lord Save Psalm 20:9

Jehovah 'Immeku – The Lord Is with you Judges 6:12

The Master's Words for Healing

Jehovah 'Izoz Hakaboth –Lord Strong and Mighty Psalm 24:8

Jehovah Jireh – The Lord Will Provide Genesis 22:14

Jehovah Kabodhi – The Lord My Glory Psalm 3:3

Jehovah Kanna –Lord Whose Name is Jealous Exodus 34:14

Jehovah Keren-Yish'i –Lord the Horn of My Salvation Psalm
   18:2

Jehovah Machsi – The Lord My Refuge Psalm 91:9

Jehovah Magen – The Lord, the Shield Deut. 33:29

Jehovah Ma'oz – The Lord . . . My Fortress Jeremiah 16:19

Jehovah Hamelech – The Lord the King Psalm 98:6

Jehovah Melech 'Olam – The Lord King Forever Psalm 10:16

Jehovah Mephalti – The Lord My Deliverer Psalm 18:2

Jehovah M'gaddishcem – The Lord Our Sanctifier Exodus 31:13

Jehovah Metsodhathi – The Lord. - My Fortress Psalm 18:2

Jehovah Misqabbi – The Lord My High Tower Psalm 18:2

Jehovah Naheh – The Lord that Smiteth Ezekiel 7:9

Jehovah Nissi – The Lord Our Banner Exodus 17:15

Jehovah 'Ori – The Lord My Light Psalm 27:1

Jehovah Rapha – The Lord that Healeth Exodus 15:26

Jehovah Rohi – The Lord My Shepherd Psalm 23:1

Jehovah Sabaoth – The Lord of Hosts I Samuel 1:3

Jehovah Sel'i – The Lord My Rock Psalm 18:2

Jehovah Shalom – The Lord Our Peace Judges 6:24

Jehovah Shammah – The Lord is There Ezekiel 48:35

Jehovah Tiskenu – The Lord Our Righteousness Jeremiah 23:6

Jehovah Tsori – O Lord My Strength Psalm 19:14

Jehovah 'Uzam – The Lord Their Strength Psalm 37:39

Jehovah Yasha – The Lord Thy Savior Isaiah 49:26; 60:16

93

Pursuing the True Living God

Thy Father of Heaven and Earth,

You are the Most Holy God, the Alpha and Omega,

the Beginning, and the End, there is none like You.

The Lord said I am thy shield, and thy exceeding great

reward. Lord I pursue You with my soul, For my soul

longeth, yea, even fainteth for the courts of the LORD:

my heart and my flesh crieth out for the living God.

But the Lord is the true God, He is the living God,

and an everlasting King: at His wrath, the earth shall

tremble, and the nations, shall not be able to abide His

indignation. From this day forward, I will pursue the

Lord.

Gen 15:1, Psalms 84:2, Jeremiah 10:10, (KJV)

94

Renouncing What Is Not Yours

Thy Father of Love and Peace,

Lord give me discernment to know, what is good or evil for me.

O Lord, I choose to let go of what does not belong to me. For the

Lord is my help and if the Lord before me then who can be against

me. I take authority in the name of Jesus, standing on the word of

God. I renounce anything that the Lord, has not given me let all

bitterness, and wrath, and anger, and clamour, and evil speaking be

put away from you, with all malice. Lord, I will trust in the Lord

with all thine heart, and lean not unto thine own understanding.

But I will trust God all the days of my life.

Ephesians 4:31, Proverbs 3:5 (KJV)

95

The Spirit of Procrastination

Heavenly Father,

It is written: 'Man shall not live by bread alone, but on every word,

that comes from the mouth of God. Spirit of procrastination,

I take authority over you right now; in the mighty name of Jesus

Christ. You have no power over me. I will do the will of the Lord

concerning me and all my assignments for this day will be

completed. Spirit of procrastination I curse you to your roots.

You will no longer be active in my life. for I will move speedily

doing the will of God concerning me, my family and all that I am

involved in. for the Lord will give me strength and power.

I will accomplish all that God has equipped me to do; through the

power of the All Mighty God. Spirit of procrastination I bind you

now, you must cease to exist right now. I am delivered from the

spirit of procrastination, I move quickly on my assignments, I take

charge over what I must complete. I maneuver through

assignments and complete them all in a timely manner by

the power of God. Spirit of procrastination, you have no effect on me, or my assignments in Jesus name, Amen. Matt 4:4 (NIV)

96

Completing the Assignment at Hand

O Mighty God,

For I am persuaded, that neither death, nor life, nor angels, nor principalities, nor powers, nor things present, nor things to come, but none of these things move me, neither count I my life dear unto myself, so that I might finish my course with joy, and the ministry, which I have received of the Lord Jesus, to testify the gospel of the grace of God. Therefore, my Lord, I ask that you give me power, and equip me to do the task at hand. I decree and declare, that I will complete the assignment at hand. not by might, nor by power' but by the spirit of the Lord. Spirit of the Lord, rain fresh on me and empower me to accomplish this assignment. That the Lord has put before me this day. I claim this assignment finished in the mighty name of Jesus Amen.   Romans 8:38, Acts 20:24 (KJV)

97

The Blessed House Prayer

Everlasting Father,

You gave me this house, now my Lord I pray You bless

it. Let sickness never touch my door post.

Let Your lovingkindness be with this house forever.

I decree and declare that this house is blessed. And there

is no perversion in it. **As for me and my house, we will**

serve the Lord, Amen.

PRAYER.
conversations with God

98

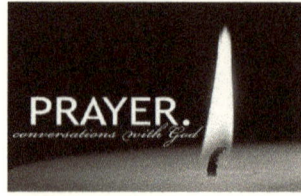

The Celibacy Prayer

Thy Father of Love,

I make a conscious decision to live celibacy this day,

and I vow to the Lord, to consecrate my body as a living sacrifice

holy and acceptable unto the Lord. For in the time of trouble,

He shall hide me in His pavilion: in the secret of His tabernacle

shall He hide me; He shall set me up upon a rock. Then my coronal

man shall be subject, to the Spirit of the Lord. I will no longer be a

slave, to the spirit of lust. And now shall mine head, be lifted up

above mine enemies round about me: therefore, will I offer in His

tabernacle sacrifices of joy; I will sing, yea, I will sing praises unto

the Lord. Hear, O Lord, when I cry with my voice: have mercy

also upon me, and answer me. When thou saidst, Seek ye my face;

my heart said unto thee, Thy face, Lord, will I seek. Hide not thy face far from me; put not thy servant away in anger: thou hast been

my help; leave me not, neither forsake me, O God of my salvation.

For I make myself available to You, have Your way in my life

this day and forever more. The word of God, is His grace,

the law of the Lord is perfect, converting the soul: the testimony

of the Lord is sure, making wise the simple.

The statutes of the Lord are right, rejoicing the heart: the

commandment of the Lord is pure, enlightening the eyes.

The fear of the Lord is clean, enduring forever: the judgments

of the Lord are true and righteous altogether.

More to be desired are they than gold, yea, than much fine gold:

sweeter also than honey and the honeycomb.

Moreover, by them is thy servant warned: and in the keeping

of them there is a great reward. Who can understand his errors?

cleanse thou me from secret faults. Keep back thy servant also

from presumptuous sins; let them not have dominion over me: then

shall I be upright, and I shall be innocent from the great

transgression. Let the words of my mouth, and the meditation of my heart, be acceptable in thy sight, O Lord, my strength, and

my Redeemer, Amen.   Psalms 19:7-14, Psalms 27:5-9 (KJV)

99

Decree and Declaring over your life

Thy Father of Glory,

I decree and declare that God is the Most High God.

I decree and declare that I speak prophetically.

I decree and declare that when we believe the Lord,

he credits it to us as righteousness.

I decree and declare nothing is too hard for the Lord.

That no weapon formed against me shall prosper.

I decree and declare The Lord is the God of Abraham Isaac,

and Jacob, as He blessed them so, shall He bless me.

I decree and declare there is no other god like you,

O Lord? You are majestic in holiness, awesome in glory,

and a, working wonders.

I decree and declare God brought his people in and planted

them on the mountain of his inheritance.

Now I am planted like a tree, that cannot be moved.

I decree and declare that the gates of hell shall not prevail against me, for if the Lord is on my side then who can be against me. I decree and declare I consecrate myself to be holy for the Lord is holy. I decree and declare what the enemy meant for my bad God have turned it around for His good. I decree and declare that the presence of the Lord will go with me, and He will give me rest. I decree and declare that God's plan is being established in my life. I decree and declare among those who approach God he will show himself holy, and in the sight of all the people, God will be honored. I decree and declare that the Lord broke the bars of my yoke and enabled me to walk with my head held high. I decree and declare the Lord bless me and keep me; the Lord make his face shine upon me and be gracious to me; the Lord turn his face toward me and give me peace; for this reason, I vow to love the Lord. I decree and declare the Lord God has blessed me in all the work of mine hands. I decree and declare that the Lord proclaimed I myself will tend my sheep and have them to lie down, declares the Sovereign Lord. I will search for the lost and bring back the strays. I will bind up the injured and strengthen the weak, but the sleek and the strong I will destroy. I will

shepherd the flock with justice. I decree and declare the day of the

Lord is near for all nations. As you have done, it will be done to

you; your deeds will return upon your own head.

The Lord teaches me how to do good deeds all the days of my life.

I decree and declare the Lord my God is with me,

He is mighty to save. He will take great delight in me,

He will give me peace with His love, He will rejoice over me with

singing. I decree and declare by God's grace,

we have the inestimable privilege, of knowing true greatness by

following our Lord in the path of servant-hood to others.

I decree and declare the things that God, has prepared for

those who love him are beyond human comprehension and

imagination and for this, I trust and believe in God.

I decree and declare it is so; I decree and declare it is the power

of the Most High God. I decree and declare God's will,

shall be done, I decree and declare Jesus is Lord,

I decree and declare it is established Amen.

100

The Good Stewardship

Thy Father of Order,

Heavenly Father I enter into Your, gates with Thanksgiving,

and into Your courts with praises.

I bless Your Holy Name all the days of my life.

I will worship You in spirit and in truth.

Have mercy on me that I may stand before you,

and mankind to be a good stewardess over all that

You have allowed me to govern.

I decree and declare that I will wake up praising

God all the days of my life and shun evil.

For You are my God and I love You, Amen.

101

Letting go of My Significant Other

Thy Father of Peace,

God thank You, for the power to let go of my significant other.

I thought it was good for a while but I thank You that You showed

me the true person they are. I know now today that they have no

rights to my life, for the harm, hurt and pain they have caused me.

I decree and declare that I speak in faith, to forgive them in the

mighty name of Jesus. Now my Lord, as I have forgiven them,

I asked You to forgive me, create in me a clean heart and renew a

right spirit. Shine down Your blessings on me, let me forever be in

Your favor. I pulldown any unclean thoughts in my mind, body

and soul. I am transformed into the likeness of Jesus Christ and I

will do good all the days of my life. God, I surrender all to You

have Your way in my life in Jesus Mighty name, Amen.

102

The Spirit of Confusion and Doubt

Thy Spirit of Truth,

I bind up the spirit of confusion, because God has given

me a sound mind. Confusion get out of my life.

Confusion get out of my mouth. confusion get out of my mind.

You have no power over me, I am a child of the Most-High God.

joint heirs with Jesus Christ. I will not doubt what God has told

me.

I will not hinder the promises of the Lord in my life.

but I will go forward and launch into my destiny and

I will do great and wonderful things in the land of the living.

because I serve a true and living God, and He shall not let me

down but He will accomplish everything that He has set for me in

Jesus name, Amen.

103

The Strength of the Lord Prayer

Thy Father of Mercy,

The strength of the Lord is mine, the Earth and all that

there is in the earth belongs to God.

When I think of the goodness of the Lord,

and all that he has done for me, my soul shout Hallelujah.

My mind, and soul praise God.

My body begins to rise and give God glory.

I raise my hand and say Thank You, Lord.

For Your strength, Thank You, Lord, for Your mercy.

Thank You, Lord, for Your grace.

You are a good God. You are a merciful God,

and there is none like You.

Holy, Holy, Holy is the Lord God Almighty, forever and ever.

The One Who Is and Was, and is to Come, Amen.

The

Peace

Prayers

104

Peace for Jerusalem

Thy Father of Heaven and Earth,

Thank you, God, for the peace of Jerusalem.

Thank You, God, for Your protection is in Jerusalem.

I read in Your Word where it says, to all that bless Jerusalem

You will bless, and them that is against Jerusalem

You will be against them, Hallelujah.

Pour down your blessings in Your protection over Jerusalem.

Jerusalem have always been the apple of Your eye,

and Because of Who You Are. I want to thank You.

For Your lovingkindness for Jerusalem.

Thank You, God You are a promise keeping God.

And the Gentiles shall see thy righteousness,

and all kings thy glory: and thou shalt be called by a new name,

which the mouth of the Lord shall name.

Isaiah 62:6 (KJV)

105

Peace in Foreign Countries

Heavenly Father,

Thank You, Lord, that I am in this foreign Country.

Thank you for Your protection. thank You for your love kindness.

Thank You, for Your grace, Thank You, for Your mercy,

and Your protection. Grant me peace in the place.

Peace in our Country. Protect me and my family,

protect them that have government-ship over me,

and grant me favor, in the land of the living.

Reveal the purpose in this Foreign Country for Your Glory.

Let me rise every morning to give You honor, Glory and

Thanksgiving, Now, therefore, ye are no more strangers and

foreigners, but fellow citizens with the saints, and of the household

of God; Amen.

Ephesians 2:19 (KJV)

106

Peace in My Spirit

Thy Father of Peace,

Is anything too hard for the Lord? Get thee behind me,

Satan and all them that worship you for it is written,

thou shalt worship the Lord thy God,

and Him only shalt thou serve.

For my peace come from the Lord not that the world gives.

From what I receive from God this world can't take from me.

For my peace comes from the Lord, Thank You God.

My God let this peace rain in my heart all the days of my life.

For I decree and declare that there is peace in my spirit therefor

I give all glory and praise unto The Lord, Amen.

107

Peace and Mercy in the Court Room

Thy Father of Righteousness,

I come to Your Holy Throne, bow down in spirit and truth

the best way I know how. My God I am asking You to forgive me

of all my sins, blot out my transgressions.

Hide not your face from me, but deliver and have mercy on me

in the time of need. give me favor with the judge.

Give me peace about this situation, and protect me,

all the days of my life. You are my judge, have mercy on me

and judge me in Your righteousness and Your love kindness

save my soul, O give thanks unto the Lord; for He is good:

For His mercy endureth forever. Amen.

Psalms 118:29 (KJV)

108

Peace in the Home

Thy Father of Love,

How merciful is Your loving-kindness, how strong are Your

Powers that no man can withstand? For You are the God that

created heaven and earth. I pray my Lord that You grant me peace

in the home.

Not the peace that this world gives me, for I am restless and my

strength is growing weak, have mercy on me, O Lord come rescue

me. For with You, comes the peace that passes all understand

Therefore, I know I can endure all things. In Jesus name, Amen.

109

Peace on the Job

Thy Father of Peace,

I Think You God, for the peace that You give.

This world didn't give me this peace,

but this peace comes from God. You Yourself is Peace my God.

I thank You, Lord, for the peace that I have in my mind, body

and soul. Have Your way in my life today, Amen.

110

United States of America Prayer

The Great I AM,

God hath made me to laugh, so that all that hear will laugh with me.

For the Lord will have favor on the United States of America, for the righteous of the land will live in peace.

They that are smitten by night will only see for at the appointed time in life. God will answer their prayers.

For the Lord has seen a great injustice in the land and He finds no pleaser in the dead. For them that says where is the Lord that created the heavens and earth with no iniquity in their hears He will hear their cry and answer their prayers.

Lord, let United State become strong and mighty in numbers,

Amen.   Gen 21:6 (KJV)

111

The Deliverance for Israel

Yes Lord,

Bless the Lord oh my soul, and forget not His benefits.

Bless His Holy name and all that He does in heaven and earth.

For the Lord work is good and He will deliver Israel in the time

of trouble. For the day of Deliverance is here for Israel.

Thank You, Lord, for Your grace, thank You for Your mercy.

All Praises belong to You, save this address in Israel.

let Your angels in camp around the doorpost of this place,

and let me forever walk in victory, prosperity, and healing

in Jesus, Mighty name. Amen.

112

The House Blessing

O Mighty God,

Bless this house O my Lord, bless the soil that this house is built

on. Bless the material of this house.

My God protect the lives that are under this roof.

Let your favor be at the doorsteps forever.

Let your mercy surround the doorpost.

I decree and declare that this place shall become a haven.

For, thou art my hiding place; thou shalt preserve me from trouble;

thou shalt compass me about with songs of deliverance.

Selah. In Jesus, mighty name, Amen.

Psalms 32:7 (KJV)

113

Victory in the City and the State

Thy Father of Hope,

Victory in the city, Victory in the state, I have Victory in this city,

and Victory in this state.

Hallelujah to Your Holy name thank You God,

for this victory thank You God, for this city and state.

I want to praise Your Holy name because You are God

all by Yourself.

I decree and declare, that I have victory in this city and I have

victory in this state in Jesus Mighty name, Amen.

114

The Blessed Church

Thy Father of Grace,

The blessings of the Lord are in this place,

the blessings of the Lord are in this church.

The blessings of the Lord are with his people.

Holy, Holy, Holy is the God that saves, You're a Righteous God.

Your Grace passeth all understanding,

today I thank You for the blessings in this church.

My Lord, continue to bless us, continue to keep us,

multiply us in great numbers, that we may raise a voice in this land

and let this church where You, have placed Your Name, be a place

of healing, deliverance and breakthroughs Hallelujah,

in Jesus name, Amen.

115

Victory in Debt Cancellation

Thy Father of Peace,

Trust in the Lord with all thine heart; and lean not unto thine own understanding. Thank you for eliminating the debts in my life, Thank You, God, because You are God, All by Yourself, and without You my God, nothing is possible; but with You my God all things are possible. I trust and believe in Your word my God. I look not at the numbers of tomorrow. For today I am set free. standing on Your word for You delivered me. You have canceled this debt, my God and because of Who You are I give You glory Your Word says owe no man anything, but a salutation. So, I thank You God, for this debt cancellation. I Thank You, for Mercy and Grace have Your Way, Give me power my God, to never assume a debt again, but my God to pay it in full in Jesus mighty name. Thou art my hiding place; thou shalt preserve me from trouble; thou shalt compass me about with songs of deliverance. Selah. Amen.   Proverbs 3:5, Psalms 32:7 (KJV)

The Prayers That Break The Spirit Of Fear

116

Fear Disappointment and Rejection Deliverance

Heavenly Father,

Disappointment and rejection is terminated in my life.

I walk in the spirit of love, I'm walking in liberty.

God have mercy upon my soul, for the disappointment

that is in my life. I cast all my cares upon You,

My God, for I know that You care for me; but every rejection

in my life, my God I thank You for bringing me through it.

For every door being closed in my face my Lord, I thank You for

slamming the door in my face, because I know my God You, have

great things for me and for all that I will ever be.

I put my trust in You and my hope is not in vain.

From this day forward, I do not fear the spirit of disappointment

and rejection, for I am delivered in the Mighty name of Jesus

Christ. Hallelujah and glory to Your Holy name, I declare that

disappointment and rejection has no power in my life, Amen.

117

The Hindering Blessings

The Mighty One,

Thank You, God, for not blessing me then, but I'm able to receive my blessings today. My own actions cause You, my God. not to bless me. Forgive me of all my sins and I forgive anyone that has sinned against me. therefore, my word is my bond and I pray that the power of the Most High God, go before me and open doors that no man can close and close all the doors, that will cause me to stumble and fall. Thank You, for my hindering blessings, for now, I am at peace

I have a good heart and I'm Focus on the Will of God concerning my life, therefore, every hindering blessing come forth in Jesus name. Heavenly Father, shower Your blessings down on me my God from Heaven, that I may know that You are the true and living God forever. Deliver me Lord right now I pray, Amen.

118

The Leading of the Holy Spirit

Holy Spirit have Your way,

Holy Spirit you are welcome, Holy Spirit illuminate this place with God's Love. The Spirit of Love consumes me. My God Your Word says the steps of a good man, is ordered by the Lord. From this day forward, I become sensitive to the Spirit of the Lord. Spirit of the Lord, lead and guide me into truth; that I may be equipped in power, to do the Will of the Lord, concerning me and my family and all that I am involved in. Holy Spirit have Your way in Jesus mighty name, Amen.

119

The Money Management Skills Spirit

Everlasting Father,

Thank You, Lord, for equipping me with a money managing skill.

Thank You, for allowing me this position.

I thank You, my God, that You have given me the wisdom to make

the money, work for me, and not me, work for the money.

for money is essential to completing the will of God. but it has no

power over me. For I possess the power over money, now money

is drawn to me daily, because of the anointing and Power on my

life. Concerning the assignments and contracts, I am involved in

this day.

I decree and declare, that I have witty ideas and inventions.

I have a billionaire money managing skills, to empower mankind

to overcome some poverty in their lives. I put all my trust in the

Lord, for He cares for me, and I thank You, Lord. For this spirit of

money managing skills. Lord have Your, way I surrender all that I

am in Jesus Mighty name, Amen.

120

The Spirit of Fear Broken

Heavenly Father,

The spirit of fear is broken, in my life. I decree and declare,

that I do not have the spirit of fear. For God has not given me,

the spirit of fear, but of love, peace and a sound mind.

I will not fear; what man can do to me; but I will reverence and

trembling of what the Almighty God is able to do to all things.

I trust You, God, I love You, Lord. Spirit of fear be gone.

For I walk, upright before God, and I will do the will of the Lord,

concerning me in Jesus Mighty name.

Spirit of fear you are terminated in my life.

In Jesus name, Amen.

121

The Strategy Prayer & Success

Heavenly Father,

I thank You, for Your faithfulness and Your promise they are dependable forever and ever. But thou shalt remember the LORD thy God: for it is he that gives thee power to get wealth that he may establish His covenant which he swore unto thy fathers, as it is this day. The LORD will send a blessing on your barns and on everything you put your hand to. The LORD your God will bless you in the land he is giving you. The LORD will establish you as his holy people, as he promised you on oath, if you keep the commands of the LORD your God and walk in obedience to Him. Then all the peoples on earth will see that you are called by the name of the LORD, and they will fear you. The LORD will grant you abundant prosperity in the fruit of your womb, the young of your livestock and the crops of your ground, in the land he swore to your ancestors to give you.

The LORD will open the heavens, the storehouse of his bounty, to send rain on your land in season and to bless all the work of

your hands. You will lend too many nations but will borrow from

none. The LORD will make you the head, not the tail. If you pay

attention to the commands of the LORD your God that I give you

this day and carefully follow them, you will always be at the top,

never at the bottom. Do not turn aside from any of the commands,

I give you today, to the right or to the left, following other gods

and serving them. I declare and decree, that I will love God with

all my heart, Amen.

Deut. 8.18 and 28.8-14 (KJV)

122

Tormenting Strongholds

Thy Father of Peace,

Spirit of the Living God, hear the words of my cry.

Let Your favor be upon me, Let the spirit of the true, and living

God rain down on me. let your anointing flow through me

uncontaminated, and unhindered.

Every tormenting spirit, I command you to dry up in the name of

Jesus. Every stronghold spirit I break, destroy, and curse you to

your roots. All tormenting, and stronghold Spirits is now deceased,

and destroyed through the Power and the Blood of Jesus Christ.

Every evil assignment in my life is terminated, and it would never

prevail. Spirit of tormenting, and strong holes you have no power

from this day forward. I cancel you and all your spirits in my life.

In Jesus Mighty name, Amen.

Grab a Prayer & Hold on Tight

The

Ministry

Prayers

123

Calling on Gabriel for the Messages

Thy Father of Provision,

calling on Gabriel, the archangel, the messenger of God.

Come down off your Watchtower, intercede on my behalf

that I may know, the words of the Lord.

For the message of the Lord shall be delivered through

you Gabriel and I shall receive; the message of the Lord to honor

it.

I will accomplish my assignment and fulfill the assignment.

Through the power and strength of the Most High God.

In Jesus Mighty name, Amen.

124

Calling on Michael the Archangel

The God of War,

Thank You God, for Michael the Archangel, You,

created him for Warfare's and Conquest in the mighty

battles for Your people in the land of the living.

I thank God for the order of Heaven, now Michael the

Archangel intercede on my behalf, promptly come down

off your Watchtower to fight for my victory.

Kill and destroy everything that is not the Will of God

concerning me for this day. I insert my name _____

in the Heaven rims, Archangel stand and declare the Word

of the Lord in heaven and in Earth and footnote it in hell.

That Satan himself may know that God is still on the Throne in

Jesus mighty name, Amen.

125

Commanding the Winds

Thy Father of Glory,

You made the winds of the East, West, North, and South.

Let Your will be done on earth as it is in heaven.

Let them blow, from the four quarters of heaven.

My God You have given us power, to command even the winds.

I take authority in Jesus name. I am commanding the winds,

in the power of God, come forth in the natural world.

I speak prophetically, to the East, West, North and the

South Winds of the Earth. Go forth concerning the will of

God for me this day that I may achieve, all that God has set

for me this year. Winds, go forth concerning my family, and

assignments. That I may accomplish all that the Lord has for me.

East wind, destroy all that come against me.

Grab a Prayer & Hold on Tight

Spirit of the Lord bring forth Your wind, by the power

of the Most High God. I call upon the wind of the Lord

East wind bring judgment upon them the judge me wrongly.

North wind replenishes all that has been lost.

South wind redirect all that God has inline for me.

West wind bring peace in my life,

that I may do the will of God, Amen.

126

Cutting the Ribbon on Gods House

Thy Father of Love,

Thank You, Lord, for this house You have placed Your

name in this house. and we give You honor, glory,

and Praises. We Thank You, God, we're getting ready to

cut the ribbon, on this house, my God. We dedicate,

this house to Your will and Your glory. We surrender all that

we are to You, because of who You, are we give You glory,

we give You praise. it's in Jesus Mighty name. We pray, Amen.

Let Your, Will, be done, concerning this house all the days

of the land of the living. In Jesus Mighty name, Amen.

127

Nurturing the Vision

Thank You, Lord,

And the LORD answered me, and said, Write the vision,

and make it plain upon tables, that he may run that read it.

Lord, I Thank you, for the vision. I thank you, Lord,

that You gave me the strength to nourish the vision;

to bring it to pass. That Your, Divine Will may come forth;

My God. Let Your Will concerning the vision come to past,

in the Mighty name of Jesus. Lord bless the vision,

God, we love You, we give You the honor,

we give You the glory, and we give You the praise.

Hallelujah, Hallelujah, Amen.

Habakkuk 2:2

128

Pray to Partner with a Ministry

Thy Father of Peace,

You are the God of Peace, You, are the God of Victory;

You are our God. We come before Your Holy Throne,

trusting, and believing that You know all things;

We ask You, my God, if we should partner with

Ministry name _____.

For when we stand together all things are possible.

When Ministries divide it is hard for the flock to follow the

shepherd. Now, my Lord, You, are a good shepherd; so,

we are coming in agreement asking that You bless the Ministries.

That we may become partners, doing great and mighty things,

in the land of the living. That this dying world may know that You

are the true and living God. In Jesus name, Amen.

129

Prayer for the Pastor

Jehovah Shalom,

Jehovah 'lzoz Hakaboth, the strong and mighty God.

Adonai, You, are our God, and we trust in Your word.

We come together and pray for the pastor. That You would lead,

guide, and direct, Like never before. Lord, send a fresh anointing,

let Your power fall fresh on the pastor. my God let the preacher

preach a Rhema word. Give Your people what they need according

to Your will and Your way. Let the pastor preach, deliverance,

and let deliverance come forth. Let the pastor preach healing,

and let healing come forth. My God, let the pastor preach

salvation, and let salvation come forth through the Holy Spirit.

Lord manifest this place like never before. Let Your gospel be

preached and let Your people be set free. whom the son sets

free is free indeed, Amen.

Psalms 124:8 (KJV)

130

Speaking the Word of God

Thy Father of Glory,

Show me, how to speak Your Holy Word. My God,

show me how to say what thus said the Lord. Give me strength,

and power to speak Your Words. Let Your Word be manifest in

my life, and in this place. Because of who You are, we give You

glory. We decree and declare, that You are the true, and living

God.

I decree and declare, that the presence of the Lord, will go with

me.

I decree and declare, that God plans, will be manifested in my life,

and evidence will appear in the land of the living, Amen.

Long time, therefore, abode they are speaking boldly in the Lord,

which gave testimony unto the word of his grace,

and granted signs and wonders to be done by their hands.

As You was with Your servants in the old,

so, shall You be with me, Amen.   Acts 14:3 (KJV)

131

The Choir's Prayer

Thy Father of Peace,

Have respect, therefore, to the prayer of thy servant,

and to his supplication, O LORD my God, to hearken unto

the cry and the prayer which thy servant prayeth before thee:

Let this prayer enter Your Holy Throne.

Let our choir sing praises unto Your Holy Heaven.

I pray, when Heaven hear the songs of this choir,

heaven rejoices for the Praises unto the Most High God.

The Lord will give strength unto his people;

the Lord will bless his people with peace.

2 Chronicles 6:19, Psalm 29:11 (KJV)

132

The Co-Pastor and Minister Prayer

Thy Father of Heaven and Earth,

I come to You Lord, knowing that all power belongs to You.

I pray for our congregation, that Your present abide in this

place as long as it is established. I pray my Lord that You move

in this ministry, like never before. Do great and mighty things

in the land of the living. We will careful give You the Honor

and the Glory in the precious name of Jesus, Amen.

133

The Deacons Prayer

Thy Father of Love,

Thank You, for our deacon board. Thank You, for our church.

Thank You, for our pastor. Lord govern this place with

Your word, with Your power and with Your strength my God.

I decree and declare that we will stand for Holiness,

Righteousness, and Love, in Jesus name, Amen.

134

The Members Prayer

The Great I AM,

All praises belong to God, You, are Alpha and Omega,

The Beginning and the End, the First and the Last.

 I thank You for my membership in this place.

Let Your will be done in Jesus name,

Open doors that only You, my God can open.

Teach me to Love as You do.

Let my membership forever be in Your glory,

Heavenly Father, as I walk in this ministry,

let my gifts, make room for them-self.

Teach me to walk in honor and dignity

all the days of my life. In Jesus Name, Amen.

Revelation 22:13

135

The Missionary Prayer

Thy Father of Mercy,

I speak prophetically over all missionaries,

My God that Your will shall be done, in the land of the living.

Thy Father of Love, teach us to deliver a Rhema Word;

that is in season. Open the hearts of Your people.

Let them see that You are the only true and living God.

Let us missionaries lay hands on the sick, Let Your healing flow

through us as it did your servant Paul. Let all sickness that we

encounter be healed. Lord raise the dead that has not Your Holy

Spirit. Shake the earth and speak life and not death in all situations.

Prophecies of the Most High God concerning all missionaries.

Empower us to accomplish Your will. Let Your will be done,

Lord. Let Your power come in this place, let it come, Lord let it

come in the Mighty name of Jesus. protect them every step of the

way. Give us power, and equip us, to do the divine will

of You Lord, in Jesus Mighty name, Amen.

136

The Mothers-Board Prayer

Thy Father of Holiness,

Unto thee, O Lord, do I lift up my soul. O' my God,

I trust in thee: let me not be ashamed, let not mine enemies

triumph over me. Show me the way to serve on this motherboard;

teach me to lead by example. Amen.

Psalm 25:1

137

The New Members Prayer

Prince of Peace,

Shew me thy ways, O' Lord; teach me thy paths.

For I am a new member in this place. My foot standeth in an even

place: in the congregations will I bless the Lord. I will trust the

Lord all the days, of my life. Amen.

Psalm 25:4 Psalm 26:12 (KJV)

138

The Pastor's Prayer

The Holy One of Israel,

My God, I am honored that You have given me this position.

I will do good all the days of my life, and I have shunned evil.

I will lead, Your people by a good example.

I will teach them Your Word, all the days of my life.

Thy Word is a lamp unto my feet and a light unto my path.

O' my Lord teach me to give light, to them that sit in the dark,

and in the shadow of death, to guide our feet into the path of peace

Now my Lord, I decree and declare that I speak Your Words

Show me how to lead Your people to stand mighty and do great

Things in the land of the living. Amen

Psalms 119: 105, Luke 1: 79 (KJV)

139

The Provision Prayer

Wonderful Counselor,

The vision is set for a time, and I the Lord will provide for the vision. Do not look to the right, nor to the left, but keep your focus on Jesus. I will cause them, that have not the spirit of the lord to bless you. I the Lord your God, will cause them that have no knowledge of you, to bless you. because I Am, the true and living God. Without Me, you can do nothing. But with Me, all things are possible, to him that believes. Now, if you shall believe the words, of the Lord. Then the prevention will, come forth in Jesus Mighty name, Amen.

140

The Vision Prayer

Thy Father of Provision,

My God, I thank You for the vision, that You put in my spirit but

this vision is a great vision, it is the Lord's doing and it is pleasing,

in my eyesight, now my God, I pray that You bring the vision to

pass. I pray my God that Your will is done concerning this Vision.

I pray my God, that we do Great and Mighty things for You.

My God, You, allowed, us to start a good deed for You,

and You my God shall accomplish all that You have started.

No weapon formed against me, shall prosper and all them that help

me, concerning this Vision my God. I pray that You. bless them,

and anyone that comes to a hindrance for me concerning this

Vision. My God, I pray that You, cripple them in their soul.

I pray my God that You will paralyze them, from speaking an evil

word concerning his vision. My God, I trust and believe that

You already worked this out for my good.

I give You glory and praise, Hallelujah.

Casting

Down

Strongholds

141

Casting down the International Spirits

Jehovah Nissi,

Holy, Holy, Is the Lord God Almighty, the One who is,

and was, and is to come. Jehovah Misqabbi,

the Lord my high tower, no international spirit of darkness,

shall govern my activities in the rim of the living.

I am a child of the Most High God.

I am joint heirs with Jesus Christ,

I am contagiously blessed up to four generations.

No international spirits shall corrupt me,

my family or anything that I love.

International spirits the Lord rebuke you.

Leave my family and me, along by the powers of the

Most High God. I cancel every activity of international spirits

Interfering in the will of God for my life; from this day forward.

You have been terminated and will never overtake me.

For Jehovah, Chezeq is the Lord my Strength, Amen.

142

Generational Curse

Thy Father of Peace,

Have mercy on me, O'Lord for You are my God.

Rejoice in the Lord, righteous ones; for the praise of the upright is beautiful. With the lyre, give thanks to the Lord; with the ten-stringed harp, play music to Him; with a new song, sing to him; with shouts of joy, play skillfully. For the word of the Lord is upright; and all his works are done in faithfulness. He loves righteousness and justice; the world is filled with the gracious love of the Lord.

By the word of the Lord the heavens were made; all the heavenly bodies by the breath of his mouth. He gathered the oceans into a single place; He put the deep water into storehouses.

Let all the world fear the Lord; let all the inhabitants of the world stand in awe of Him; because he spoke and it came to be because He commanded, it stood firm. The Lord makes void the counsel of nations; he frustrates the plans of people.

The Master's Words for Healing

But the Lord's counsel stands firm forever,

the plans in His mind for all generations. How blessed is the

nation whose God is the Lord, the people He has chosen as

His own inheritance? When the Lord looks down from heaven,

He observes every human being. Look! I'm about to grant you a

blessing and a curse. A blessing if you obey the commands of the

Lord your God, that I'm giving you today or a curse if you don't

obey the commands of the Lord your God, by turning from the

that I'm commanding you today and following other gods whom

you have not known. Now decree the blessings and follow my will.

I decree and declare that God grants me and my family

supernatural, strength with the ability to fight the good fight of

faith. God qualifies us to share in the inheritance of Jesus Christ,

reconciling us with God. I decree and declare, that we are firmly

rooted and established by God. I decree and declare, that healing

powers flow through us to lay hands on the sick, and they shall

be healed. We are anointed by God.

There is a hedge of protection around us, we are ambassadors for Christ. We are armed with multiple-billion-dollar ideas and inventions. Heavenly Father, equip us to expose Satan's tactic to overcome his attacks. In Jesus name, Amen.

Psalms 33: 1-13, Deuteronomy 11:26-28. (ISV)

143

The Spirit of Calamity

Thy Father of Love,

Spirit of calamity, I bind you up, in the mighty name of Jesus.

I take authority in Jesus name, the spirit of calamity,

you have no Power over my life. Dry up, and die.

In the Mighty name of Jesus. I decree and declare,

that the day of the Lord is near for all nations.

My God Proclaim my victory in this season.

Because You are my God and I trust in You, Amen.

144

The Spirit of Hate

Thy Father of Love,

I decree and declare, the spirit of hate you have no power

in this life. I have made my supplications known,

unto the Most High God. He will deliver me in the time of need,

He will carry me from the East to the West, the North and the

South, with His Mighty Power. I will walk boldly in the Spirit of

the Lord, and I will say until the spirit of hate.

I transform you into the spirit of love,

I cancel every hate thought in this body.

I cancel and Destroy every evil mind and thought

concerning the will of God.

Spirit of love annihilates the spirit of hate. I am about my father's

business, for this is the day that the Lord has made,

I will be glad and rejoice in it Spirit of the Lord.

Spirit of hate be gone in the Mighty name of Jesus.

145

The Spirit of Lack

O' Lord,

Thank You for Your grace and mercy. Make a joyful noise unto the Lord, all ye lands. Serve the Lord with gladness: come before His presence with singing. Spirit of lack I bind you up in the Mighty name of Jesus. For I lack no good thing, God is my provider. Spirit of lack get out of my life. In the name of Jesus, Amen.   Psalm 100:1-2

146

The Spirit of Lust and Pride

My Lord,

Spirit of lust and pride I bind you in the name of Jesus,

Get out of my body, get out of my heart and mind.

O' Lord God, to whom vengeance belongeth; O God,

to whom vengeance belongeth, shew thyself. Lift up thyself,

thou judge of the earth: render a reward to the proud.

Show forth Your Mighty strength in this place.

I decree and declare that lust and pride will not possess me.

Lord forgive me of all my sins, blot out all my transgressions,

and teach me Your way. In Jesus Mighty name, Amen.

Psalm 94:1-2

147

The Spirit of Racism

Thank You, God,

Spirit of racism, I curse you to your roots.

I destroy every evidence of racism in this place.

I wipe out every thought of prejudice, prejudgment and racism

In the mighty name of Jesus, Satan you don't win.

My God is King and Lord of all. Spirit of Racism

Get your thoughts and actions out of my mind body and soul.

I plead the blood of Jesus over me, this place,

and all that I love. Lord let racism die,

let it never prevail in this situation.

My God You are Jehovah Jireh, deliver in a time like this,

and destroy the spirit of racism, provide My Lord,

protection for them that racism tries to claim.

In Jesus name, Amen.

148

The Spirit of Witchcraft

Thy Father of Mercy,

Spirit of witchcraft, I come against every Warlock,

every Witch. I cancel every assignment of any voodoo that

anyone has put on me or over me. Witchcraft has no power

over me are anything that is concerning me and my family.

I destroy every sorcery activities in my home, land, and workplace.

In the Almighty name of God, The Great I Am;

the Alpha and the Omega, Satan the Lord, rebuke you

concerning me, and all that I'm, and will ever be involved in.

I cancel every assignment that witchcraft has in my life.

I cancel every plot that any Witch or Warlock has tried to use to

control me, with the blood of Jesus. I plead the blood of Jesus

over me and all that I will ever be. I create a blueprint of my life

up to four generations. The blueprint mandates, that no weapon

formed against me shall prosper. and anyone that comes against

me that is not the will of God; He will condemn.

I serve fair warning in the Earth and footnote it in hell.

That when you come against the Almighty God.

Your reward will be death. Lord have Your way in this

situation in Jesus mighty name, Amen.

Prayers

For

Protection

149

The War Prayer

Thy Father of Truth,

Lord, I Thank You, that we are fighting for what is right.

Teach us Your way, that we may follow.

Lead us in the path of righteousness.

Let no harm or death come near our doorstep.

Protect us through this war and deliver victory in the

Mighty name of Jesus, Amen.

150

The Children Protection in School Prayer

Thy Father of Love,

Let no harm, or chaos come near our doorpost.

Protect us all the days of our life. Let no weapon formed

against us prosper, for our trust is in the Lord.

The Great I Am, the Alpha and the Omega,

the Beginning and the End. The one who is, and was,

and is to come. Holy, Holy, Holy is the Lord God Almighty.

Thank You, my God. For protecting us in this school.

Thank You, my God, because Your word cannot come back

to You void. Heaven suffer violence, and the violence take it

back by force, Thank You, Lord, for our protectors Amen.

(Know Your Enemy)

151

The Enemy Prayer

Thy Father of Glory,

I walked upright in Your sight. Now my enemies are

throwing stones and hiding their hands; they smile in

my face and shed my blood. O, my Lord, how long will

You look on the wicked and be still. My soul has no rest

for my eyes, hide not Your face from me, lend ear unto my call.

My enemy is at my door, look upon their evil deeds.

Vindicate me O Lord for I put my trust in You.

Forgive me of all my sins for I am weak.

Hear a just cause; O Lord attend to my cry.

Give ear to my prayer which is not from deceitful lips.

Let my vindication come from Your presence.

Let Your eyes look on the things that are upright,

test my heart and put Your approval on me.

The Master's Words for Healing

Arise O Lord and comfort me. I have loved the habitation

of Your house and the Place where Your glory dwells.

Do not gather my soul with the sinner nor let me live with

bloodthirsty mankind. They have planned schemes to destroy

me and dishonor Your name. For I am one, that proclaims

Your Glory I testify of Your marvelous works. I call upon

Your name in the midst of the land for they know that

I keep your commandments for every commandment

You have made to keep order in the land.

The evildoers have made a covenant to sow deceitfully

and have enlarged their false testimonies to destroy

Your everlasting name. Your Word says You, hate every false

way and they that false witness shall perish

my Lord, it is written; Do not fret because of evildoers nor

be envious of the workers of iniquity for they shall soon

be cut down like the grass and wither as the green herb.

Lord, I have committed my ways to You,

I have trusted in You and my deeds are good.

Grab a Prayer & Hold on Tight

I have waited on You, hurry my Lord my enemies are rising as

fast as the sun comes up and the moon goes down.

Forgive me of all my iniquities I am pleading my case.

 I have delighted myself in You. O Lord and You shall

give me the desires of my heart. Lord give me peace in

abundance. Heal my broken bones and cleanse my heart and soul;

let me never be ashamed let no famine rest at my door,

let deceit never come from my lips.

Your protection is on those who keep Your commandments,

Your, mercy O Lord is in the earth and heavens.

Your faithfulness reaches to the most inner parts of mankind soul.

Your righteousness is like the red sea. Your judgments

give life and death. Let me live and not die.

I am the seed of Abraham let Your covenant be with me also,

bless those who bless me and curse those who curse me.

Those that bless me make them a blessing to others,

those that desire evil for me; my Lord let evil return

unto their hearts seven-fold. Remember then that harms me

without a cause, let no rest enter their tent. Let them not inherit

the fruit of their labor nor profit from evil deeds.

Let sickness claim their temple, oh my God outstretch

Your arm and show them the calamity of the wicked.

My Lord my God; I am crying out to You, because of my affliction,

my sorrow seems to be increasing the multitude

of my enemies' iniquities day by day. Now my Lord speak on my

behalf

those who plunder me my Lord let them be a plunder,

all who prey upon me make them a prey.

Them that devour me, my Lord, my God let them be devoured

let all of my adversaries be thrown into captivity let their eyes

be bloodshot red because You said. Do not touch my anointed,

and do my prophets no harm. O my Lord my God my life is in

Your hands if You don't rescue, me I won't be rescued.

If you don't deliver me My Lord my God my soul will surely

go to the grave. Now my Lord if this pleases you take my soul today.

For I shall live with you forever. I surrender all to You.

Grab a Prayer & Hold on Tight

I pray for my enemies when their hearts turn to You have

mercy on them. Let Your will be done on earth as it is in heaven.

 I will forever give thanks to You. O my Lord my God for You are

good. Your mercy endures forever, You, are Lord of lords and King

of kings there is none like You. Your wisdom is unsearchable;

Your loving-kindness reaches to all generations.

You will deliver me O Lord from all my enemies.

For You are the lover of my soul, I put my trust in You.

Honor and glory belong to You, May You live forever

and ever, Amen.

152

The President Prayer

Thy Father of Grace,

Have mercy on our land, I pray for the president Lord,

let them lead with integrity, let them govern this place with

dignity.

I pray that no wrong is found in their heart.

I pray that the presidential leadership is in Your, Will Lord.

I pray that if there is anything, not pleasing to You my God,

in the president heart bring it to their attention and govern them

to correct it. That their service may be pleasing to You Lord.

That they may worship You in Spirit, and in Truth.

Teach them to lead with authority and compassion all the days

of their life. Expose the tactics of our enemies.

Prepare them to fight the good fight of faith.

To do good for our land let them be recognized for

honor and grace, let these be the words of the Lord forever.

To God be the glory, Amen.

153

Traveling Grace

Excellent is the Name of the Lord,

I pray for traveling grace Lord, Your Word says

no harm will overtake you, no disaster will come near your tent.

For he will command his angels concerning you to guard you

in all your ways; they will lift you up in their hands,

so that you will not strike your foot against a stone.

I pray for this journey my Lord,

accomplish all that You have set before me.

I pray for traveling grace that as I exit and enter

my destination all shall be well in Jesus Mighty name, Amen.

154

The Military Prayer

My God,

You are my protector, I put my trust in You. Lord,

Protect my family why I am away.

Let them know that I serve for our country.

Let my family be at peace. Let mercy be on the right, and

let grace be on their left. Lead them into all truth.

Show me how to be a great example in the military.

Protect me, my God, nevertheless I'm not afraid of death;

To God be the glory. Now my God,

I serve that we may have the right to love You,

to praise You, and to honor You, and to live in peace.

I promise, to uphold all the rights, in the Military,

in my everyday life; to do good all the days of my life, Amen

155

Protection from Terrorism

Thy Father Peace,

Terrorism is all in the nation, but You my God can deliver us.

You are my God that protects. You are the God that deliver,

and we look for no other God but the God of Israel,

the God of Jacob, in the God of Abraham.

We thank you for being our God.

Shine down your glory in this place,

I summons the Archangel Michael,

come down off your Watchtower and fight on our behalf,

protect us in the mighty name of Jesus, Amen.

156

Pray the Storm Away

Thy Father Mercy,

I can see clearly through this storm,

I see myself pressing forward going to the end.

I am empowered with the word of God.

and this storm shall not overtake me, nor shall it harm me.

But it is only a test, for my God will get the glory through

this storm. For this storm have come,

that I may set my house in order. For as the Lord live;

I will do it according to His will, all the days of my life.

I will stand for justice, I will uphold the righteous,

and I will be granted breakthroughs in this storm.

For I know, it's only a test, and I shall pass the test, Amen.

157

Thieves in the Work Place

The Father of Truth,

Let them that still, in the workplace be revealed.

Let the traps, that they set for their enemies.

Let them fall back in their own traps.

Let the spotlight shine, on them that take from this place;

Bring them to shame. I Thank You, Lord, in advance,

for Your provision, Your protection,

and for Your Love Hallelujah, Amen.

158

Commanding the Enemy

Thy Father of Victory,

Give me power, to decree and declare, a word and my God

bring it to pass. I decree and declare, that the enemy tricks are

terminated in my life. I decree and declare, that every assignment

the enemy has sent forth, to destroy me is canceled, in Jesus name.

I command the enemy, to pay back one hundred folds;

what you have stolen from me. Give back my health,

give back my peace, give back my victory,

and give back my money. for I command you enemy,

to return everything that I lost, in Jesus Mighty name, Amen.

159

The Protection of my Environment

Thy Father of Grace,

I come in the name of Jesus, in the volume of the book.

I speak prophetically. I decree and declare that God is Lord.

I pray for heavenly protection over this environment.

I pray Heavenly Father, that You, my God,

will govern this environment. Heavenly Father,

I pray that no harm would come to this place.

Thank You in advance for Your Miracle, Signs,

and Wonders in the land of the living, Hallelujah,

Amen.

160

The Readers Prayer

Heavenly Father,

I pray that You, protect them, all the days of their life.

Let no weapon formed against them ever prosper.

Let every tongue that rises against them, be put to shame

Heavenly Father, You, are just and faithful to forgive.

have Your way in this readers life.

Heavenly Father make the crooked places straight,

give them peace that passes all understanding.

We give You glory, honor, and praises in the Mighty name of

Jesus.

Grab a Prayer & Hold on Tight

The 50
States
Global
Prayers

161

The Alabama Prayer

Thy Father of Love,

I pray for Alabama, I pray my Lord that You cover the state of
Alabama with Your grace and mercy. I pray for our governors
that are in authority to do good unto the people. I pray that you
give them the heart of Christ to lead righteously. And let us
consider one another to provoke unto love and to good works:
Open avenues for Your people, close the doors that will cause
Alabama to stumble. Open channels of restoration, highways of
recovering. Shine Your light on the hate crimes that they may be
prosecuted and let Your loving-kindness rain on Alabama. Let
them know that we are a city of peace and righteousness. For we
will rise up against all corruption and injustice that You're, will
may be done. Thy Father of Love govern the mayor heart of

Alabama to do good and not evil for the people Amen.

162

The Alaska Prayer

The Father of Glory,

Thank You for Alaska, thank you for the moon and the stars.

Thank You, Lord, for the fresh air that we breathe.

I pray for the mayor of Alaska that peace rain at their door all the days of their life. I pray that the danger that creeps around the corners be assassinated; Lord let them that have power over Your people reign in righteousness, let their hearts be attentive to the Holy Spirit. Lord neutralize the gang Banging and eliminate the racism. Close the doors to criminal escapades that Your people may live and not die. For we will seek ye first the kingdom of God and all his righteousness and all these things shall be added unto you, Amen.

163

The Arizona Prayer
The Great I Am

Have mercy upon Arizona, my Lord secure employment to the land of Arizona. Bring forth, righteous enterprises and development to grow Arizona that we may live comfortable and not perish.

Let them that have authority improved State policies. My God, You, are righteous in all that you do. Enforce CFED to promote better Financial Security to alleviate poverty. Let the minority of the people have favor in Your sight. For we know, But the humble will inherit the land and will delight themselves in abundant prosperity;

in Jesus name, Amen.

164

The Arkansas Prayer

Thy Father Peace,

I pray for Arkansas, Lord Stop the violence. Cut off the hand that oppresses Your people. Destroy them in government that rules injustice. Bind satanic harassment, and rebuke the leaders that govern without compassion. Help Arkansas be a light in a dying world.

Let us come together, and grow in a mighty nation, Amen.

165

The California Prayer

Thy Father of Love,

I speak that God's anointing destroys every uncleaned yoke in

California. Lord decrease the aggravated assault, dismantle

all violent crimes. Execute all rapist, cancel the high percentage

of homicides in our city. Reduce the gang violence.

Make California a blessed place. California is well-known for its

warm Mediterranean climate. From this day forward let California

be known for a State that honors God, and worship You, my God,

in spirit and truth. Let the governor of California, know and

trust in God. Let the children of California, be taught the word

of God. Let them stand for righteousness, and holiness all the

days of their life. Let their children, children know that there

is a God in heaven that heals, save and deliver, Amen.

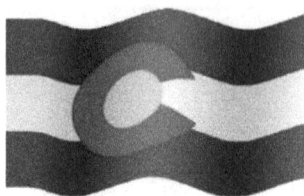

166

The Colorado Prayer

Thy Father of Peace,

Annihilate the property crime in Colorado,

rain down your blessings in this place, let all thieves be arrested,

and prosecuted to the fullest of the law. My God,

let no assault go unpunished. Raise up a banner for Your people,

that we may know that You are a true and living God;

and that You, my God, have not forsaken Colorado,

teach our children, to do Your will, all the days of their life,

Amen.

167

The Connecticut Prayer

Wonderful Counselor,

I speak prophetically, against any habitation of burglary,

and theft. discord any assignment of aggravated assault.

Heavenly Father let Larceny cease in Connecticut.

My God You are Jehovah Keren-Yish'i.

The Lord is my light and my salvation, whom shall I fear.

I put all my trust in You Lord, Amen.

Psalms 18:2 (KJV)

168

The Delaware Prayer

Heavenly Father of Love,

Blessed are the undefiled in the way, who walk in the law

of the Lord. My God established Delaware to be a strong state.

Stop the burglaries in our city, and cancer every vehicle

vandalism on the streets. Destroy them that practice in

vehicle theft activities. That our city may stand for what is good,

and acceptable in the eyes of the Lord, Amen.

Psalms 119:1

169

The Florida Prayer

Heavenly Father of Heaven and Earth,

I decree and declare, that the drug trafficking must obliterate in

Florida. Demolish the kidnapping, Lord and protect the innocent.

Council and save them that have become victims of human

trafficking. Decrease the property crimes. Rob them that commit

crimes. That they may know, that there is a God in Florida,

that saves, delivers, and heals in the time of trouble.

In the Majestic name of Jesus Christ, Amen.

170

The Georgia Prayer

Heavenly Father of Grace,

Georgia cries out, to You because You are our God.

Lord put a halt to the aggravated assault,

give us the spirit of wisdom, that we may worship You,

in spirit and truth. Send judgment to them that rape,

and bring justice, to all that have been burglarized.

Show the mayors of Georgia how to rule Godley.

Let Southwest Georgia, not be ranked as the fourth poorest

in the nation. Thy Father of Love, improve our children education.

That Georgia youth may grow up, to be prominent citizens.

Teach me, O Lord, the way of thy statutes; and I shall keep it

The Master's Words for Healing

unto the end. And we know that all things work, together for good,

to them that love God, to them who are the called,

according to His purpose, In Jesus name, let all that Love God

say Georgia is blessed, Amen.   Psalm 119:33, Romans 8:28

171

The Hawaii Prayer

Thy Father of Love,

Deal bountifully with thy servant, that I may live, and keep Thy Word. Open thou mine eyes, that I may behold wondrous things out of Thy Law. Lord quicken the property crime to bring it to a halt. Stop the man slaughtering in Hawaii and destroy them that rape. Let them that have family be a beacon of light and hope in this place, let Hawaii authorities govern in righteousness, Lord let all that love Hawaii love You, Amen.

Psalm 119:17-18 (KJV)

172

The Idaho Prayer

Thy Father of Righteousness,

Stop the bank robberies, protect the Boise Police Department,

as they follow Your laws. Dear Lord,

show them that You are a good, and merciful God.

Cancel ever murder-suicide in this land. Let them that rape,

be robbed of their freedom.

Give us the power, to stand in holiness and righteousness.

Give us the wisdom to rise above poverty.

That we may do great things in Idaho,

in Jesus, Mighty name, Amen.

ILLINOIS

173

The Illinois Prayer

Yes Lord,

Have mercy on Illinois, my God, teach us to do your will in

our state. Oh, Lord, there is so much killing.

It is becoming normal; You God, see all things,

have your way in Illinois.

Raise up Your people to remove the people that are

causing harm to Illinois.

Give them a sense of urgency to do good and not evil.

Hide not Your face, from our call, for we are Your people

my God. The state of Illinois is crying out to You, for who shall

deliver us, but a God Like You. You, my Lord, can cause the

vandalism to cease, You, can stop the robberies.

You are a great God, You, are a merciful God, You,

The Master's Words for Healing

are our healer, You, are our saving God. Deliver us,

for such a time like this.

God have Your way in the state of Illinois.

Let Your people know, that You have not forgotten us.

Let all senseless killing stop.

Illinois trust, and believe in Your, Holy Word,

and we count on You my God, for our deliverance,

healings, and our breakthroughs. Heal,

deliver and save my God. Let us come together,

to mend the broken hearts. That we may build up Illinois,

to the place You would have it to be.

That they may know, that You are a true and living God.

Bless our City, that we may be able to train, the officials to

escalate a problem, more peacefully;

and keep all our official safe, and holy to do good,

for the people of Illinois, and not evil, Amen.

174

The Indiana Prayer

Thy Father of Peace,

Thank You, Lord, for Your protection over Indiana.

Thank You, Lord, for Your grace and mercy.

Watch over our leaders. Heavenly Father, show us how to fight,

for educational funding. Show us, my Lord, how to let no dysfunctional policy maker, rule over us. You're God all by Yourself, and without You my God, nothing is possible. Indiana is trusting and believing in You Lord. Protect our children, open doors for great opportunities. For them that are standing, according to Your will, and Your way. Raise us up to walk, in dignity and love in Jesus name, Amen.

IOWA

175

The Iowa Prayer

Thy Father of Truth,

My God, You, are all Love. Cancel the murdering with the people,

build Iowa to be a land, where Your love flows.

Stop the crooked politicians, give us my God, better health care

plans. Give wisdom to them that govern Iowa, teach them to

govern in power and love. In Jesus name, Amen.

176

The Kansas Prayer

Heavenly Father,

Make Kansas, a money managing skills resource center.

Stop them that commit and practice arson.

Let them that commit homicide be judged fairly.

Prosecute all that use racist and sexually graffiti to entrap

our people. Let the children of Kansas be known for honorable

things, in the land of the living.

Let us love You with our whole heart.

Let all that live in Kansas love the Lord. Amen.

177

The Kentucky Prayer

The Mighty One,

My God, You, have decreased the property crimes in Kentucky.

Now, my Lord, I pray that You decrease the violent crimes in our

streets. That they may become peaceful and walkable again.

Teach us to love You, God, as You love Kentucky.

Let this state be a place where Your people will find refuge,

in Jesus name, Amen.

178

The Louisiana Prayer

Thy Father of Glory,

Louisiana was named in the honor of the late King Louis XIV,

The King of France form 1643-1715, but today my God, You,

are still God the sets on the throne. You look down on Your people

and You bless them. For Your word says. But my God shall

supply all your need according to his riches in glory by Christ

Jesus. Let Mardi Gras claim none of Your children lives.

Let the witches, and the warlocks' activities, have no authority

over God's people, I decree and declare that all witches and

warlocks power cause no harm. My God let all the voodoo dolls,

power have no effect render them all powerless in Jesus Name.

Because You are God with all Power, and You my God,

will never die, Amen.   Philippians 4:19 (KJV)

179

The Maine Prayer

Heavenly Father,

Stop the sexual assault in Maine. Prosecute them that rape,

break the neck of the gang power.

Thy Father of love, uphold Maine in Your righteousness.

I decree and declare that we will become a state that loves God.

I decree and declare that Jesus is Lord.

I decree and declare that the citizens of Maine

will praise God forever, Amen.

180

The Maryland Prayer

Thy Father of Love,

Govern the streets of Baltimore, dismantle the robberies,

bring equal justice in the legal system. I will praise Thee;

for I am fearfully and wonderfully made: marvellous are thy

works; and that my soul knoweth right well. Bring justice to Your

people

my God. Teach our children, to do Your will.

For I proclaim, You, Lord, is the God of Maryland.

In Jesus name, Amen.

Psalm 139:14 (KJV)

181

The Massachusetts Prayer

Heavenly Father,

Thank you, for Your grace. Thank You,

for Your mercy and Your lovingkindness;

that endures to all generations. Heavenly Father,

thank You for Massachusetts crimes reducing.

Stop all them that commit crimes in Massachusetts,

cause destruction to them that cause destruction to Massachusetts.

Lord, I pray for our children, to be at peace,

with one another, that they grow up,

and learn who You are God.

I pray that them, that govern Massachusetts will be able,

to do, the will of God.

In Jesus Mighty name, Amen

182

The Michigan Prayer

Thy Heavenly Father,

Teach us, the laws of Michigan my God.

That we may honor them in knowledge, and truth.

Thy Father of all power, show Michigan that You are God.

That You sit high and look low, show us that You judge the

righteous and reward them that do good. and my God,

You, judge the unrighteous and reward them their deeds.

Teach us how to forgive, and teach us how to forgive ourselves.

Show us how to live for You, all the days of our life.

Let our children call us blessed, and let mankind know,

that Michigan is a place that God dwells, Amen.

183

The Minnesota Prayer

Prince of Peace,

Let all human trafficking, come to a halt. Disallow violent crimes,

property crimes, terminate the theft and burglaries in Minnesota.

Show politicians how to govern with compassion.

Show forth Your right hand, in all power. That we may know,

that there is a true, and living God in Minnesota.

Increase the job opportunities, protect the homeless.

Show Your, children, who You, really are, my God.

So as You was, with the children of Abraham;

so shall you be with the children of Minnesota, Amen.

184

The Mississippi Prayer

Heavenly Father,

Govern the roads and highways of Baltimore Let no robberies
claim the lives of Your people, Change the law to be equal for all
people, in Mississippi. For Your word says; Howbeit in vain do
they worship me, teaching for doctrines the commandments of
men. For laying aside the commandment of God, ye hold the
tradition of men, as the washing of pots and cups: and many other
such like things ye do. And he said unto them, Full well ye reject
the commandment of God, that ye may keep your own tradition.
Teach us my Lord to worship You in spirit and in truth.
Let no corruption lay at our doorpost. Let Mississippi forever
give You praise in Jesus name, Amen.

185

The Missouri Prayer

Thy Father of Love,

Lord guide and protect us all the days of my life,

teach the children of Missouri to do Your divine will.

Open the doors of opportunity for education, that our youth may

stand with wisdom and power. Stop the drug trafficking,

empower Missouri to eat and live healthier that we may become

mighty men and women of God in the land of Missouri.

Show forth your Mighty power let your blessings be in this land

forever, let no terror overcome Missouri, instruct Missouri them

to change, the world to do good and not evil.

Give them the wisdom to stand in power,

doing the will of God in Jesus mighty name, Amen.

186

The Montana Prayer

Thy Father of Love,

For the LORD is our defense and the Holy One of Israel

is our king. Montana loves you God increase Iowa Employment

stop the human trafficking destroy them that commit property

crimes we decree and declare that meant Anna it's a place where

God bless you are Elohim God the strong creator you are

Jehovah Ez-Lami the Lord my strength.

I decree and declare that the Lord will bless Montana

I decree and declare that Montana will establish the will of God

for our state, I speak that God anointing will destroy

The yoke of depression in Jesus name, Amen.

Psalms 28:7, Psalms 89:19 (KJV)

187

The Nebraska Prayer

Thy Prince of Peace,

The Great I Am the Alpha and the Omega Nebraska trust in

You for we claim You to be the God of Nebraska cease

aggravated assault and larceny-theft in Nebraska;

bring to an end cybercrime in our state.

Jehovah Mekaddishkem,

speak thou also unto the children of Israel, saying,

Verily my sabbaths ye shall keep:

for it is a sign between me and you throughout your generations;

that ye may know that I am the LORD that doth sanctify you.

Allow us to come together and worship You in spirit and truth,

Amen.   Exodus 31:13 (KJV)

188

The Nevada Prayer

Heavenly Father,

Conclude pandering, and sex tariffing. Break the neck of violent

crimes and property crimes in the land of Nevada.

Speak Love to Nevada and have mercy on our land. For we have

made prostitution legal in the land of the living.

For Your word say; My son, attend unto my wisdom,

 and bow thine ear to my understanding: That thou mayest regard

discretion, and that thy lips may keep knowledge.

For the lips of a strange woman drop as a honeycomb,

and her mouth is smoother than oil: But her end is bitter as

wormwood, sharp as a two-edged sword.

Her feet go down to death; her steps take hold on hell.

The Master's Words for Healing

Lest thou shouldest ponder the path of life,

 her ways are moveable, that thou canst not know them.

Hear me now, therefore, O ye children,

and depart not from the words of my mouth.

Remove thy way far from her, and come not nigh the door

of her house: Lest thou give thine honour unto others,

and thy years unto the cruel: Lest strangers be filled with thy

wealth; and thy labours be in the house of a stranger;

And thou mourn at the last, when thy flesh and thy body are

consumed, and say, how have I hated instruction,

and my heart despised reproof; And have not obeyed the voice

of my teachers, nor inclined mine ear to them that instructed me!

I was almost in all evil in the midst of the congregation and

assembly.

Proverbs 5:-14 (KJV)

189

The New Hampshire Prayer

Thy Father of Love,

Terminate the random killing, let us be mindful of educating our children. Specially the day that thou stoodest before the LORD thy God in Horeb, when the LORD said unto me,

gather me the people together, and I will make them hear my words, that they may learn to fear me all the days that they shall live upon the earth, and that they may teach their children.

Give us providence employment, that New Hampshire may stay vibrant, and resourceful, in Jesus name, Amen.

Deuteronomy 4:10 (KJV)

190

The New Jersey Prayer

Heavenly Father,

O' merciful God, wash me thoroughly from mine iniquity,

and cleanse me from my sin. For I acknowledge my

transgressions: and my sin is ever before me. Against thee, thee

only,

have I sinned, and done this evil in thy sight: that thou mightest

be justified when thou speakest and be clear when thou judgest.

Demolish the drug addiction, establish safe havens for the

authorizes that protect and serve with integrity,

for New Jersey trust in the Lord, Amen.

Psalms 51:2-4 (KJV)

191

The New Mexico Prayer

Thy Father of Peace,

Let Your blessings be with Mexico.

Rain down Your anointing,

in this place. Let everyone that lives, in Mexico says

Jesus is Lord. Cancel the murdering on our land.

Dismantle the drug abuse, and destroy all that commit crimes

in human trafficking. Let Mexico be a place where the

troubling can find rest. Thy father of Love,

let not the waters of Mexico claim the

lives of anyone that declares Jesus is Lord, Amen.

192

The New York Prayer

Dear God,

Jehovah-Jireh, You, are the God that sees all,

You, are the God that provides, for them that loves You.

Hallelujah to the King of Kings, Hallelujah to the Lord of lords.

Glory be to the Almighty God; the God of New York.

Heavenly Father, destroy them that kill without a cause,

blind them that look upon pornography let the pictures have no

effect. Teach us that Your Will is always better for all mankind.

Open New York eyes that we may see the beauty of the Lord.

Shame them that practice in cybercrimes, let their systems crash

and let them lose all that is precious to them. Let it be known that

New York is not as cold-hearted is the world seem to think.

For the people of New York, stud in the time of trouble

as we did in nine-eleven. So, shall we will come together,

to declare that there is a God. The God of Abraham, Isaac,

and Jacob; is the same God of New York. for in times like this,

we need a Saviour, Amen.

193

The North Carolina Prayer

Thy Heavenly Father,

Raise up a banner, against the organized crime.

Show forth Your Mighty Power. Wipeout gang-related crimes.

Let North Carolina equal rights shine on all mankind.

Permit North Carolina to stand, and declare that God is, a good

God. That delivers in the time of need, and when trouble arises. He

shall protect them that love Him. Lead, and protect, our children,

bless our families that stand for righteousness. Empower us to live

holy, and righteous all the days of our life. In Jesus Mighty name,

Amen.

194

The North Dakota Prayer

Thy Father of Peace,

My God move Mighty on North Dakota, lay hold on drug-related crimes. Prosecute to the fullest and stop the murderers, in their tracks. Let them know my God, that they can never give a life back. Manifest a glimpse of what their life, would be like if they kill. It's not just the motion of pulling the trigger. It's the torment that destroys peace. Lord before their eyes blink twice; give the people a sense of urgency of life, before taking someone else life, because someone, may take the life of someone you love.

Let North Dakota be conscious, of the carjacking, and the motor-vehicle crimes that are committed, in North Dakota. Bring it to a halt my God, empower us to educate one another, to do the will of God that North Dakota May stand in righteousness, Amen.

195

The Ohio Prayer

Thy Father of Love,

The Father of Abraham, The Father of Isaac, and the Father of

Jacob. You are the God that lives, and because You live. Today

Ohio can stand, to say Jesus is Lord.

Let all that rob in Ohio, let them be robbed, let all that commit

property crimes, let crimes be committed upon them. Heavenly

Father, raise up a nation, that please, and honor, You. Empower us

to worship You, in spirit and in truth; all the days of our life. Let

anything that is not pleasing to God, in the state of Ohio be

revealed. Bring about correction and resolution; with

commitments, to do good for the people of Ohio. Amen.

196

The Oklahoma Prayer

Thy Father of Glory,

Bring peace up on Oklahoma. let Oklahoma State stay peaceful.

Never let the bombing acts claim this land again.

Prosecute all that comes against Oklahoma. Enable us, God,

to educate our children to do Great and Mighty things in the land

of Oklahoma. Let Oklahoma become a safe haven for them that

love the Lord. I prophesy over Oklahoma,

that the streets of Oklahoma are safe, that the churches of

Oklahoma deliver, a holy word with compassion and correction

through the love and power of God. In Jesus Majestic name,

Amen.

197

The Oregon Prayer

Heavenly Father,

I pray that You bless Oregon, God is a Spirit: and they that worship him must worship him in spirit and in truth.

I declare that in the years to come, Favor will live in Oregon, let the people of Oregon be filled,

with the present of God, and praise Him forever.

I decree and declare that Oregon is spiritually, financially and emotionally blessed in Jesus name,

Amen.

John 4:24 (KJV)

198

The Pennsylvania Prayer

Heavenly Father,

Let all that love Pennsylvania say Jesus is Lord.

I declare that Pennsylvania is supernatural blessed,

by the power of God. I pray that no weapon formed,

against Pennsylvania shall prosper. Heavenly Father,

dismantle all the home robberies,

cancel the murdering in this land. Let them that commit rape,

let them become sodomized for you are the God with all power.

God have Your way in Pennsylvania like never, before.

My God the people of Pennsylvania trust and believe in You Lord,

Amen.

199

The Rhode Island Prayer

Thy Father of Hope,

Lord, Rhode Island trust in You, I believe You are working this

out for Rhode Island good. I decree and declare that the burglary,

robbery, rape and assault must obliterate in Jesus name. let Rhode

Island praise ye the Lord. Blessed is the man that feareth the Lord,

that delighteth greatly in His commandments.

His seed shall be mighty upon the earth:

the generation of the upright shall be blessed: in Jesus name,

Amen.

Psalm 112:1-2

200

The South Carolina Prayer

Thy Father of Peace,

Lord thank You for keeping South Carolina safe,

empower us to leave a legacy of hope, love and peace.

"I will say of the LORD, He is my refuge and my fortress:

my God; in him will I trust."

I plead the blood of Jesus over South Carolina and all that

we stand for in Jesus name, Amen.

Psalms 91:2 (KJV)

The Master's Words for Healing

201
The South Dakota Prayer

Thy Father of Grace,

Hide not Your Face O Lord from our cry. Attend to our prayers.

That we may know that You are a true and living God.

Downsize the aggravated assault, prosecute them that commit

property crime. Holy, Holy, Holy is the Lord God Almighty.

Let Your blessing be in South Dakota,

Let the Joy of the Lord shine like never before.

Send down Your Blessing Lord, send down Your Rain,

Send down Your Fresh anointing.

 Let South Dakota rise and declare Your Name Lord.

Let us declare, Your, Glory, and declare Your praises in the

land of the living, for You are South Dakota God, Amen.

202
The Tennessee Prayer
The father of Glory,

Holy, Holy; Holy is the Lord God Almighty.

Lord thank you for your protection in Tennessee,

cover our children my God increase the education here that

they may grow up to be great men and women. God show the

political parties to do right for the people of Tennessee let the

mayor of Tennessee be holy and upright concerning the people.

I pray for all this killing to stop in the mighty name of Jesus,

God stop the gun violence, terminate the hate crimes.

God reduce the robberies in Tennessee, downsize the child abuse;

let the parents see the value of themselves and their children.

I decree and declare that Tennessee is a great place to live

I stand upright before God with a repentant and forgiving heart

that I would do good for Tennessee and not evil

The Master's Words for Healing

I prosper in the land that I live. Tennessee will be a great place

in the land of the living in Jesus mighty name, Amen.

203

The Texas Prayer

Heavenly Father,

O give thanks unto the Lord; for He is good: for his mercy endureth forever. O give thanks unto the God of gods: for his mercy endureth forever. O give thanks to the Lord of lords: for his mercy endureth forever. To Him who alone doeth great wonders: for His mercy endureth forever. I bind all forces warring against Texas, Heavenly Father stop all cyber-crime in Texas. Stop the floods, Forgive Texas provide food clothes and shelter and save Your people.

Let us educate our children to do the will of God, teach us Your will that we may follow and worship You God all the days of our lives. In Jesus name, Amen.   Psalm 136:1-4

204

The Utah Prayer

Thy Father of Mercy,

Uphold Utah, that we may worship You in Spirit and truth.

I call forth all the treasures of Utah from the enemy.

I decree and declare that Utah is spiritually, physically,

and financially blessed.

I decree and declare that the joy of the Lord, rule,

rest and abide in Jesus Christ, for all that dwell in Utah.

For we shall find refuge in Jesus Christ, Amen.

205

The Vermont Prayer

Thy Father of Love,

Let Vermont live in peace, let our fruitfulness be the joy of the

Lord. For we will dwell in the secret place of the Most High God.

I decree and declare that restoration is in Vermont.

For we raise our young to do noble things in the land of the living.

We rise early to give God thanks. We declare that Jesus is Lord.

Heavenly Father keep us sensitive to the Holy Spirit.

That Vermont will be a place of refuge.

In Jesus mighty name, Amen.

206

The Virginia Prayer

Heavenly Father,

Virginia is a wonderful place, let all that lives in Virginia rise early to praise the Lord. Holy Spirit Virginia just wants to praise the Lord, Heavenly Father, have mercy on us. For Your mercy endures forever. Holy Spirit, move in this State. Send forth Your Mighty power that all that lives will give God glory. Praise ye the Lord. Praise ye the name of the Lord; praise him, O ye servants. Of the Lord.

Lord Continue Your blessing in Virginia that we may stand to declare You glory, Amen. To God be the Glory,

Psalm 135:1 (KJV)

207

The Washington Prayer

Thy Father of Love,

Washington is the place to be, for Your word say. Give ear,

O my people, to my law: incline your ears to the words of my

mouth. I will open my mouth in a parable: I will utter dark saying

of old: which we have heard and know, and our fathers have told

us. For Washington will trust in the Lord. We will worship God in

spirit and in truth. Force the homicide to decrease. Blind the rapist,

cripple the thief. Crush the dishonorable politicians.

Promote, them that declare Jesus is Lord.

Let the impossible become possible in Washington.

Let the politicians govern with honesty and dignity.

Let all that live in Washington praise the Lord, Amen.

208

The West Virginia Prayer

Thy Father of Mercy,

Lord, thou hast been our dwelling place in all generation.

Before the mountains were brought forth or ever thou

hadst formed the earth and the world, even from everlasting

to everlasting thou art God. We that live in West Virginia,

take authority in Jesus name, to declare that the people of God

shall be blessed with abundance. Lord cancel all motor

vehicle theft, burn out the arson, and entrap them that seek

profit from human trafficking. I decree and declare that

Jesus will supply all West Virginia needs, Amen.

Psalm 90:1-2 (KJV)

WISCONSIN

1848

209

The Wisconsin Prayer

Thy Father of Peace,

Have mercy on Wisconsin, unarm the murders, desex-arouse,

the rapist, I declare that assault, in Wisconsin,

has no effect and the power of, the assault has deceased in Jesus

name. Give unto the Lord, O ye mighty, give unto the Lord glory

and strength. Give unto the Lord the glory due unto his name;

worship the Lord in the beauty of holiness, Amen.

Teach our politicians to govern in truth, open doors of

opportunities for miracles, signs, and wonders for our children in

Wisconsin in Jesus name, Amen.

Psalm 29:1-2 (KJV)

210

The Wyoming Prayer

Heavenly Father,

I decree and declare that all brokenness, and negligent,

is been replenished by the joy of the Lord.

I confess that the spirit of confusion shall not empower over

Wyoming. Lord pass judgment upon them that rape and commit

robbery. Bring peace to Wyoming that we may serve You, in spirit,

and in truth. A thousand shall fall at thy side, and ten thousand

at thy right hand; but it shall not come night thee.

Only with thine eyes shalt thou behold and see the reward

of the wicked. For Wyoming trust and believe in God, Amen.

Psalm 91:7-8 (KJV)

The

Seven

Continents

Prayers

FLAGS OF ASIA
complete set

211

The Asia Prayer

Heavenly Father,

Lord teach the government, not to ignore organized crimes.

Empower Asia authorities to serve in dignity and honor.

Let no corruption stay covered. Let no corrupt communication

proceed out of your mouth, but that which is good to the use of

edifying, that it may minister grace unto the hearers.

And grieve not the Holy Spirit of God,

whereby ye are sealed unto the day of redemption.

Let all bitterness, and wrath, and anger, and clamour, and evil

speaking be put away from you, with all malice:

And be ye kind one to another, tenderhearted,

forgiving one another, even as God for Christ's sake hath

forgiven you.   Ephesians 4:29-31 (KJV)

212

The Africa Prayer

Heavenly Father,

You, are God, and Africa trust in You.

Our hope is not in vain, we honor You because You are God.

He that dwelleth in the secret place of the Most High shall abide

under the shadow of the Almighty. I will say of the LORD,

He is my refuge and my fortress: my God; in him will I trust.

Raise up a banner, against them that caused Africa to suffer;

for a profit. Let all that practice in human trafficking,

be enslaved in their own mind. Bring forth judgment on all that

dishonor Africa. Let the nations know, that You are the God of

Africa. Bless all mankind, that blesses Africa with water and food.

Let our children not go to bed hungry, but let them know,

The Master's Words for Healing

that You are the God that Deliver, in the time of need.

You, are the God, that Heals, You, are the God that Saves,

and You are the own Mighty God, that will deliver Africa.

For we are a country that needs a Savior, we are a country,

that our hope is not in vain. For we put our trust in You God.

For You, my Lord, will deliver us in Africa.

I decree and declare that all that brings shelters and education to

Africa shall be blessed. My God, raise up a nation that loves You,

that honors You, and worship You in spirit and in truth.

Now all that love, God shouted Amen.

Psalms 91:1-2 (KJV)

213

The North America Prayer

Thy Heavenly Father,

Let us never run out of water, let Your name be praised in North America forever, surely goodness, and mercy shall follow me all the days of my life; and I will dwell in the house of the Lord forever.

My God let North America be known for a place of peace, and not war, let our children know that You are a good God, and let all that govern, North America know that You are a God of honor, love and judgement Amen.

Psalm 23:6 (KJV)

214

The Europe Prayer

Thy Father of Peace,

I prophesied that European debt crisis has no effect on

Gods people, for we stand for holiness.

Let all child abuse, sexual assault, and robberies be caught and

prosecuted. My God clean the temples of Europe,

let no house of God be made a house of thieves.

Let wisdom and honor rest in this place.

Let the name of God be forever known, in Europe,

Amen.

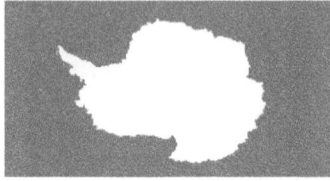

215

The Antarctica Prayer

Thy Father of Mercy,

We thank You for McMurdo Station.

We pray that You continue to keep us safe. That our mind

is stayed on God. Thank You, Lord, for Your, mercy and

Your, grace. God cast me not away from thy presence;

and take not thy Holy Spirit from me.

I decree and declare that Antarctica meltdown shall not

destroy Gods people, in Jesus name, Amen.

Psalm 51:11 (KJV)

216

The Australia Prayer

Thy Father of Love,

Thank you for being God all by Yourself, You,

are the God that created heaven and earth and there

is no other God. We choose to serve.

We plead the blood of Jesus over Australia,

no weapon formed against us shall prosper.

We terminate the spirit of kidnapping by the blood of Jesus.

We demolish the spirit of thieve and robbing and we disassemble

the spirit of molestation and terminate the spirit of killing

and murder in Australia, through the authority and power of God,

Amen.

217

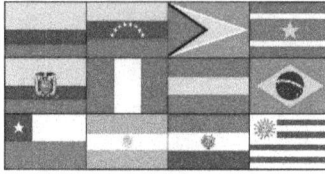

The South America Prayer

Thy Father of Grace,

Thank you for South America, Lord I pray that You stop

the muggings, carjacking, and kidnapping in South America

Paralyze the robbing, terminate the gang-related violence.

That we make know that You are our true and living God.

Thy Father of Mercy assassinate all sexual assault in

South America that one day we will rise above any crooked

politicians in the Might name of God. O' Lord grant

South America a righteous president that honor You, my Lord.

Protect the Presidential Palace when the President is doing

right by the people, Amen.

218

The Virgin Island Prayer

Thy Father of Peace,

Holy, Holy, Holy. Is the Lord God Almighty,

the one who is and was, and is to come!

My God all power belongs to You. I thank You Lord

for the Virgin Island. I pray this prayer, that You protect the

Virgin Island. Place a shield of protection around it,

and we will lift Your Holy Name Lord. Stop the domestic

violence.

Terminate the sexual arousing in the child molestation.

Heavenly Father decrease the violence and the vandalism.

Stop the thieves in their tracks and protect the land.

I fully trust and believe in Your Holy Word and I thank You in advance, for Your grace and Your mercy and Your protection, over the Virgin Islands, have Your way my God in this place in Jesus mighty name. I will be careful to give You the Glory and Honor Which You, so rightfully deserve. Hallelujah and, Amen.

219

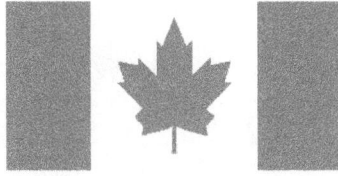

The Canada Prayer

The Father of Glory,

Have mercy on Canada, Teach as Your, Will my Lord, open doors for Canada that only You can open. Let all them that are in authority of government honor You, my God. Ceate in me a clean heart and renew a right spirit. Have Your, way in the land of the living in Canada my God, for We Trust and Believe in Your Holy Word. We stand as a people that we take authority in the Mighty name of Jesus, casting down every imagination that exalts itself above the knowledge of God. Dear Heavenly Father reduce the homicide, we bind up the spirit of depression of suicide, we decree and declare that we are whole in Jesus name and we're trusting in the Name of Jesus to deliver Canada in Jesus Mighty name, Amen.

220

The Prayer for Columbia

Thy Father of Peace,

Lord, let no corruption govern Your people.

Jehovah Jireh, provide employment in Columbia. Make a way out of no way, that Your people may be eligible to receive proper medical attention and medication. Decreased the street violence. balance the arresting that it may be fair. Let them that bring harm to Your people, let harm be at their doorpost. Stop the kidnapping, eliminate the harassment, and cut off the corruption in our land. For You are Jehovah Machsi the Lord my Refuge.

Columbia trust in You God, Amen.

221

The Puerto Rico Prayer

The God of Truth,

Heavenly Father, never let there be a Masacre de Cayey

situation in Puerto Rico Again. Lord, stop the mass quantity

of drug trafficking in Puerto Rico. Ensure our children safety,

that they may receive a good education.

Decreased the gang activities, and break the Latino gang Kings.

That Your word maybe taught and preached in the land of the

living. Protect them that stand for righteousness,

empower them to do Your will all the days of their life.

crippled the crooked politicians, cancel the enemy tricks

Let Puerto Rico not only be called the place of paradise

but let it be known for the place of peace,

in Jesus Mighty name, Amen.

222

The Pakistan Prayer

Thy Father of Love and Grace,

Have mercy on Pakistan, let us not be victim of violence, Let the World know that You Love Pakistan. Hear, O Lord, when I cry with my voice: have mercy also upon me, and answer me. When thou sadist, seek ye my face; my heart said unto thee, Thy face, Lord, will I seek. Hide not thy face far from me; put not thy servant away in anger: thou hast been my help; leave me not, neither forsake me, O God of my salvation. For my faith, is in God. Elohim Kedoshim, Holy God, El Rai the God that sees me. There is power in the name of Jesus, God empower our children to raise up and praise You. Let no Christian be beaten to death. Have mercy Lord on Pakistan. Let all that Love God help Pakistan,

Amen.   Psalm 27:7-9 (KJV)

NAMES OF GOD

Elohim-GOD (Genesis 1:1) - The strong creator
Jehovah-LORD (Genesis 2:4) -The self-existing One
Adonai-LORD/Master (Genesis 15:2)-The Headship Name
Jehovah El Elohim (Joshua 22:22)- The LORD GOD of GODS
Jehovah Elohim (Genesis 2:4, 3:9-13, 21) -The LORD GOD
Jehovah Elohe Abothekem (Joshua 18:3)- The LORD GOD of Your
Fathers
Jehovah El Elyon (Genesis 14:22) - The LORD, The Most High GOD
Jehovah El Emeth (Psalms 31:5) - LORD GOD of Truth
Jehovah El Gemuwal (Jeremiah 51:56)- The LORD GOD of Recompenses
Jehovah Elohim Tsebaoth (Psalms 59:5, Isaiah 28:22)-LORD GOD of Hosts
Jehovah Elohe Yeshuathi (Psalms 88:1) - LORD GOD of My Salvation
Jehovah Elohe Yisrael (Psalms 41:13) - The LORD GOD of Israel
El, Elohim, and Elohe (Genesis 1:1) - GOD
Elohim Bashamayim (Joshua 2:11)- GOD in Heaven
El Bethel (Genesis 35:7)- GOD of the House of GOD
Elohe Chaseddi (Psalms 59:10)- The GOD of My Mercy
Elohe Yisrael (Genesis 33:20)- GOD, the GOD of Israel
El Elyon (Genesis 14:18, Daniel 3:26, Psalms 78:56) - The Most High GOD
El Emunah (Deuteronomy 7:9 - The Faithful GOD
El Gibbor (Isaiah 9:6) - Mighty GOD
El Hakabodh (Psalms 29:3) - The GOD of Glory
El Hay (Joshua 3:10, Jeremiah 23:36, Daniel 3:26) - The Living GOD
El Hayyay (Psalms 42:8)- GOD of My Life
Elohim Kedoshim (Joshua 24:19) - Holy GOD
El Kanna (Exodus 20:5 - Jealous GOD
El Kanno (Joshua 24:19) - Jealous GOD
Elohe Mauzi (Psalms 43:2) - GOD of My Strength
Elohim Machase Lanu (Psalms 62:8) - GOD Our Refuge
Eli Maelekhi (Psalms 68:24) - GOD My King
El Marom (Micah 6:6)- GOD Most High
El Nekamoth (Psalms 18:47)- GOD that Avenge
El Nose (Psalms 99:8) - GOD that Forgave
Elohenu Olam (Psalms 48:14) - Our Everlasting GOD
Elohim Ozer Li (Psalms 54:4) GOD My Helper
El Rai (Genesis 16:13) - GOD Sees Me
Elsali (Psalms 42:9) GOD, My Rock
El Shaddai (Genesis 17:1,2, Ezekiel 10:5)- Almighty GOD
Elohim Shophtim Ba-Arets (Psalms 58:11)- GOD that Judged in the Earth
El Simchath Gili (Psalms 43:4 - GOD My Exceeding Joy
Elohim Tsebaoth (Psalms 80:7, Jeremiah 35:17&38:17) - GOD of Hosts

Elohe Tishuathi (Psalms 18:46&51:14) - GOD of My Salvation
Elohe Tsadeki (Psalms 4:1) - GOD of My Righteousness
Elohe Yakob (Psalms 20:1)- GOD of Israel
Elohe Yisrael (Psalms 59:5)- GOD of Israel
Jehovah (Exodus 6:2,3)- The LORD
Adonai Jehovah (Genesis 15:2)- Lord GOD
Jehovah Adon Kol Ha-Arets (Joshua 3:11) - The LORD, The Lord of All the Earth
Jehovah Bore (Isaiah 40:28) - The LORD Creator
Jehovah Chereb (Deuteronomy 33:29) - The LORD... The Sword
Jehovah Eli (Psalms 18:2) - The LORD My GOD
Jehovah Elyon (Genesis 14:18-20) - The LORD Most High
Jehovah Gibbor Milchamah (Psalms 24:8)- The LORD Mighty In Battle
Jehovah Maginnenu (Psalms 89:18) - The LORD Our Defense
Jehovah Goelekh (Isaiah 49:26&60:16) - The LORD Thy Redeemer
Jehovah Hashopet (Judges 11:27)- The LORD the Judge
Jehovah Hoshiah (Psalms 20:9) - O LORD Save
Jehovah Immeka (Judges 6:12) - The LORD Is with You
Jehovah Izuz Wegibbor (Psalms 24:8)- The LORD Strong and Mighty
Jehovah-jireth (Genesis 22:14 - The LORD Shall Provide
Jehovah Kabodhi (Psalms 3:3)- The LORD My GOD
Jehovah Kanna Shemo (Exodus 34:14)- The LORD Whose Name Is Jealous
Jehovah Keren-Yishi (Psalms 18:2 - The LORD the Horn of My Salvation
Jehovah Machsi (Psalms 91:9)-The LORD My Refuge
Jehovah Magen (Deuteronomy 33:29) - The LORD the Shield
Jehovah Makkeh (Ezekiel 7:9) - The LORD that Smite
Jehovah Mauzzam (Psalms 37:39)- The LORD Their Strength
Jehovah Mauzzi (Jeremiah 16:19)- The LORD My Fortress
Jehovah Ha-Melech (Psalms 98:6) - The LORD the King
Jehovah Melech Olam (Psalms 10:16) - The LORD King Forever
Jehovah Mephalti (Psalms 18:2)- The LORD My Deliverer
Jehovah Mekaddishkem (Exodus 31:13) - The LORD that Sanctifies You
Jehovah Metsudhathi (Psalms 18:2 - The LORD My High Tower
Jehovah Moshiekh (Isaiah 49:26&60:16) - The LORD Your Savior
Jehovah Nissi (Exodus 17:15) - The LORD My Banner
Jehovah Ori (Psalms 27:1) - The LORD My Light
Jehovah Uzzi (Psalms 28:7) - The LORD My Strength
Jehovah Rophe (Exodus 15:26) - The LORD Our Healer
Jehovah Roi (Psalms 23:1) - The LORD My Shepherd
Jehovah Sabaoth (Tsebaoth) (I Samuel 1:3) - The LORD of Hosts
Jehovah Sali (Psalms 18:2) - The LORD My Rock
Jehovah Shalom (Judges 6:24)- The LORD (our) Peace
Jehovah Shammah (Ezekiel 48:35) - The LORD Is There
Jehovah Tsidkenu (Jeremiah 23:6) - The LORD Our Righteousness
Jehovah Tsuri (Psalms 19:14) - O LORD My Strength

THANK YOU, LORD,

TO GOD BE THE GLORY,

FOREVER AND EVER AMEN.

All have sin and came short of the glory of God, but when you repent and forgive others that have hurt you. God open rivers of understanding and forgiveness. Once you have forgiven yourself, of all your pass sins, it's easy to move forward. By learning what God has assigned to your life, once you know that your destiny is set in motion. Fly like an eagle, Godspeed.

This book is loaded with prayers that change lives,
by the power of God Almighty. This book has over 200
powerful prayers including a prayer for all 50 States.

These prayers have unraveled, over the last ten years,
through miracles, signs, and wonders.
People receive visions of all sorts; What's your vision?
If the vision never leaves you it's essential to your destiny.
Miracles, signs, and wonders; are the Lord's promises
taken effect in your life.
Step into your inheritance with God, through the Power and
Blood of Jesus Christ our Lord and Savior.

It doesn't matter how you pray, as long as you pray with a
sincere, and repentant heart. God knows the hearts of
mankind; after all he made us all. Experience the praying
powers of the Great I AM. Jesus prayed it's our time now.

Find your situation in these powerful prayers; Prayers that
Heal, Strengthen Faith Prayers, Peace Prayers, Prayers that
Break the Spirit of Fear, Ministry Prayers, Prayers that Cast
Down Strongholds, Protection Prayers, Global Prayers
50 States Prayers and The Seven Continent, and much more.

It's time that you pray through the storms, weeping may
endure for a night, but joy cometh in the morning.
Find the prayer that matches your situation and pray until
God moves on your behalf. Prayer Changes Things!

Jesus prayed, it's your time now; pray, Pray, PRAY.

www.ingramcontent.com/pod-product-compliance
Lightning Source LLC
Chambersburg PA
CBHW021217090426
42740CB00006B/263